Pro HTML

The Frontend Engineering Series

Pro HTML

HTML 4.01
HTML5
HTML Living Standard

Martin Rinehart

Frontend Engineering I: Pro HTML

Written and Designed in LibreOffice Writer, Published to PDF, all in the USA.

Printed as near to our customers as our technology permits.

Table of Contents

Contents

Contents

Contents

Introduction

Why HTML?

HTML is the *lingua franca* of the World-wide Web. Would you like to put content online? You will want to mark it up with HTML.

HTML is not just the language used to mark up pages. Backend tools, such as Java Server Pages and the PHP language (the language of Wikipedia and, until recently, Facebook) send content to your browser. The content they send? HTML.

The client end of the Internet, formerly browsers running on computers, mostly desktop PCs, is exploding. Smartphones and tablets are browsing and running web applications. Almost all these applications are presented, whatever the device size, in one language: HTML.

We're not sure what you would like to put on the web. But we are sure what you need to learn first, to put anything on the web: HTML.

Why Pro HTML?

Writing professional HTML takes a bit more savvy but no more effort than writing amateur HTML.

Ready to learn? Let's go. It's not hard. (And, for those with allergies, it has no math.)

1 Write Your First HTML

This is a "knowit" (knowledge unit). That means (in this case) that it has an online part, as well as this print part. The online part is at:

MartinRinehart.com

(No need to type "www.".)

```
Online: Knowits > HTML I > Welcome
```

That box labeled "Online:" (we call it the "drilldown") shows you how to navigate when you get to the website. You click "Knowits" and another menu appears. You click

"HTML I" and you get to the *HTML* menu. You click "Welcome" and … Well, you probably guessed.

In this chapter you'll write your first HTML and see your first page in your browsers. It's not hard.

Right now, go to:

Online: Knowits > HTML I > Welcome

(You'll want to arrange a comfortable position where you can look at the screen and at this print. If your "print" is a PDF, printing it would be a good idea.) Start with the online explanation of a "knowit." We'll wait.

Knowit Recap

A knowit, knowledge unit, can combine media. This one combines print and online. Print is easier to read. (There are about a quarter million "pixels" in a square centimeter of this print. There are about 800 pixels in a square centimeter of a typical monitor.) But putting your mouse on the printed page and clicking is not going to get you anywhere. Both media have advantages, so we use both.

Now, off to the Companion page, the start of the knowit for this chapter:

Online: Knowits > HTML I > Online > 1

(We hope you noticed that if "Knowits" and "HTML I" were already punched, it took just two clicks to get to "Online" and then "1". The great goal of all frontend engineering: make the visitors job simple!)

Now, let's get started. Each chapter, including this one, begins with a brief "history." We start from the dawn of time but we'll get to electricity (chapter 2), very quickly. (We're big fans of history. It's a lot of fun if you don't leave it to historians.)

History—Before Electricity

Our universe (and therefore, our HTML) began with a big bang, about 15 billion years ago. Stuff went flying in all directions. Galaxies spun around. Stars congealed. Our Earth started revolving and orbiting our Sun.

Life began. Living things became plants and animals, at least one of which crawled out of the ooze to live on dry land. We got dinosaurs, then mammals, monkeys and a couple weird animals that walked on two feet: *homo erectus* and then *homo sapiens*.

If we measure this in millions of years (let's call them *megayears*), 14,999 were gone before the latest started. (15,000 will visit us again.) We'll divide the final megayear into two eras, pre-electric and post-electric. In the first era, *homo sapiens* hunted and gathered. Then he (or, perhaps more precisely, she) learned to grow crops and we got villages, cities, wars and empires. This gave us stones, bronze and iron; science and mathematics; and we began to fiddle with a strange form of energy, called "electricity."

We'll get back to this tale (with a very soggy Ben Franklin flying his kite) in Chapter 2. First, though, let's write some HTML!

http://www.umich.edu/~gs265/bigbang.htm, Age of the universe: 4.6×10^{17} seconds. If your calculator's not handy, that's about 1.5×10^{11} years.

(Remember: you can click on that link online.)

Websites—SEO

After History, we return to websites and specifically, to the planning and design work that precedes writing the first bit of HTML. For the opening chapter we abandon our normally organized approach to begin with SEO, Search Engine Optimization, the most important part of website marketing.

Marketing? Yes, marketing!

You want your website to have visitors, even if it's not commercial. If you are not prepared to pay big bucks, you want users to find your site when they search for one like it, and preferably to have your site first in their first page of search results. (Studies have found that almost no one looks at the second page of search results. Very few even look past the top half of the first page. Being number one is huge!) Search Engine Optimization, SEO, is the science and art of doing things that will get your site a top placement on the search engine results pages (SERPs).

As we discuss the various HTML tags we'll highlight those that are really important for SEO. In this chapter, we'll cover, among others, the <h1> tag. It is used for the largest (and most important) heading. It is vital for SEO. If someone searches for "whole grain cereal" and your site is about whole grain cereal you want to be sure that "whole grain cereal" (which is called, in SEO, a "keyword" even though it's a phrase) appears in your <h1> heading. Try diving into this article in the Engineers' track online:

Online: Engineers > Frontend Team > Fe SEO

If you ever expect to create the next Facebook, SEO is vital. If you want to create a good site for your hometown pizza parlor, or your friend just starting her law practice,

SEO is vital. If you are an international spy and you want to have a site that isn't listed by any search engine, good SEO can help with that goal, too. Keep your antennae tuned for every mention of SEO here and online.

Tools—Editor, Browsers

No craftsman should be without a collection of tools. If you're serious about your craft you want the very best tools available. If you want to create HTML, your very excellent tools will all be free. (You can pay more, if you insist. Some of the higher priced tools actually may have advantages. Photo editing is commonly done with Adobe tools, like Photoshop, which are very expensive. Very!) HTML tools are low-priced, if they are priced at all.

Your HTML work will be very easy to understand (if not so easy to do). You use a text editor to enter your HTML and then you use your browsers to look at the result. Let's start with a text editor.

Notepad++

On Windows, Notepad++ is an excellent programmer's editor. If the file you are editing ends with the `.html` extension (and your HTML files will) Notepad++ assumes that you are editing HTML and configures itself appropriately. In fact, Notepad++ is so rich in features but still so easy to use that we devote a separate section in each chapter to highlight one of its "secrets."

On a Mac? TextEdit, which comes with OS/X, is an excellent programmer's editor so there's no need to install anything else, but there is a reason to worry. HTML in different browsers is not quite standard. You'll need to test the various Windows browsers, which means you'll need to test on Windows. This is not a "test when you think you're done" sort of thing. It's a "test continuously, every step" to catch issues as you go along. For that reason, few HTML authors use a Mac (even though many may prefer a Mac for everything else). So if you don't have access to a Windows machine, try to arrange access to a good friend with one so you can test your work every day.

On Windows you could actually use Notepad, but you'll be kicking yourself for doing it. We'll show you, as we go along building our site, how a couple extra mouse clicks can edit several files at once. So visit

notepad-plus-plus.org

and download your Notepad++. Follow the instructions and you'll be ready to start writing HTML, which is what we do next. (By the by, the Notepad++ installer will ask you if you really want to use the old-fashioned, too-large icon on your desktop. We're still partial to that one.) And for you hopeless cynics, we use Notepad++ every day writing HTML and several other languages and get no other compensation for recommending it to you.

Browsers

With Notepad++ ready, you've got all you need to write HTML. (We'll introduce you to other tools as we go along. With Lorem Ipsum you'll be writing—sort of—good Latin!) Now you need to test your work in browsers. No, that's not "a browser," it's "browsers," plural. We recommend Google Chrome, Mozilla Firefox, Microsoft Internet Explorer, and Opera. (You can test Safari in lieu of Chrome if you prefer. They're both built on the Webkit engine, so they're very much the same when it comes to rendering HTML. "Rendering" in cooking refers to cooking off excess fat—on the web it refers to displaying the text and graphics specified by HTML on a screen or other device.)

Download any of these browsers you don't already have. (Remember, the online part of the knowit is clickable. You'll find the download links online.) Get each installed and running. If you have the monitor space, make the "Refresh" button of each available for clicking. At least organize yourself so you can "Alt+Tab" your way through the chain to pick a browser.

Hello, World!

Now let's put these tools to use. The first challenge you face using any new language (that means "new to you," not new to the world) is to make your computer correctly run a program that says "Hello, World!". So fire up Notepad++ and type "Hello, World!" on the top line. (No, there isn't really any HTML going on. Be patient.)

Save your "program" in a file named `hw.html` and file this in a folder that is quite convenient. (The name preceding `.html` is really up to you. The `.html` is almost mandatory. Back in the very old days, just after St. George slew the dragon, Windows was limited to three characters in the suffix, so `.htm` was also enabled. Don't use this unless you have armor and a broadsword in your closet.)

Now, in each browser, in turn, press Ctrl+O (or click File/Open) and select the file you just saved. Each of your browsers should now report "Hello, World!" in the top-left corner of the browser's window, which is called the "client area" of the browser.

Congratulations. You have just created and viewed a web page. No, there wasn't any HTML but you did use the two critical tools: text editor and browsers. Now let's get on to HTML.

Head

There are two parts to almost every HTML page: the head and the body. Each chapter here will have one major section, often a short one, devoted to the head section's content and two major sections, usually longer, devoted to block content and inline content, the two classic types of body content. In this chapter we'll actually begin at the very beginning, which comes at the beginning of your HTML page, just above the head section. Ready to write your first real HTML?

Beginning HTML

Let's do it! Let's add some real HTML. One of the things that separates the professionals from the amateurs is the presence of a "doctype" declaration. These used to be quite complex bits of SGML, Standard Generalized Markup Language, on which HTML was based. Fortunately, HTML5 introduced a very simple doctype, just as effective, and all browsers support it:

```
<!DOCTYPE html>
```

A note on capitalization: HTML doesn't care how you capitalize its tags and attribute names. The XHTML dialect insisted on lowercase. As lowercase is easier to type, the XHTML convention was adopted happily. We capitalize "DOCTYPE" (as you see above) for reasons that are explained in an obscure document linked in the Chapter 9 Companion page. You'll put "DOCTYPE" in a template where you'll never have to type it a second time.

That doctype declaration must be the very first thing (top line, far left) in your HTML file. We'll explain this next. For now, add it to your file, preceding the "Hello" text, and test it in at least one browser. If you haven't made a mistake, you'll see no difference.

Online: Knowits > HTML I > Online > 1 > 1a

When it is time to try something online we'll have an example on the online portion of this knowit. You can look at the example if you need help. The drilldown tells you that you should be doing something online.

If you haven't done so, yet, back up to `<!DOCTYPE html>` and add the doctype to your `hw.html` page. View the page in a browser or two. Look at example 1a in another browser. Got it?

Now arrange your browsers in some order that you like. You want to cycle through them in order. (Ours are alphabetical.) The idea is that you will continuously test in each of the four so that if issues crop up (and they will!) you are never very far from the cause of a problem.

Why a Doctype?

In the bad old days, all browsers were different. All browser vendors used a different subset of HTML, added a proprietary collection of extensions and hoped that you would write HTML specifically for their browsers and not for the competitors. This became unbearable back at the end of the last century.

So all browser vendors started working together (more or less) in standards committees to create a standard HTML. (Our History lessons will cover this in more detail.) And they invented modes: "standards" modes (in which they were all supposed to operate the same way on standard HTML) and "quirks" modes (which was whatever way they had been going on their own, in the bad old days). Adding a doctype really is a directive to the browser: "I'm writing in standard HTML, so behave yourself! No quirks allowed."

We will show you how to create a template from which you will start all your HTML files. The template will start with a doctype, of course, so you will never actually create any quirks mode pages. (Unless, of course, you are curious. Quirks mode does not make your computer start to emit smoke. At least we hope it doesn't. We haven't tried in years.)

Blocks

Now, on to our first block tags. We'll cover tag basics here, then four block tags divided into just three sections (as the last two are inseparable).

A tag is the basic HTML construct. To start your first and most important heading, for instance, you use the `<h1>` tag, this way:

```
<h1>This Is the Most Important
Heading</h1>
```

More on the `<h1>` heading in just a bit. For now, we'll examine tags in general. All tags are enclosed in angle brackets. (They are just above the comma and period on a standard western keyboard. Get used to them as you'll type lots of angle brackets.)

Most tags come in pairs, one opening and the other closing. The opening tag suggests its type. The most common are the most terse. `<h1>`, for example, is a very terse way of saying "the most important heading." The closing tag is identical to the opening except that it inserts a forward slash just inside the opening angle bracket: the <h1> starts the heading, the </h1> ends it. Now on to our three block groups, after a word about the terminology.

HTML5, including the Living Standard, does not use the terms "block" and "inline." It distinguishes between "flow" content and "phrasing" content. These are (roughly) the same as our block and inline content. The newer terms will mislead you in older browsers, such as MSIE 8. The older terms still work in all browsers, so we'll stick with them.

<h1>**Most Important**</h1>

The <h1> tag pair surrounds your most important heading(s). Time to try one?

Online: Knowits > HTML I > Online > 1 > 1b

That was the drilldown. You said to yourself, "Self! Time to try this online!" And you did so. Right? (Warning: reading these words without doing the online work is really a waste of time. Would you learn to play tennis without swinging a racket and hitting a ball?)

When you write an <h1> heading, you are writing the item that will attract your visitor's immediate attention. Choose your words carefully. When you follow our examples in your learning files, be creative! If the lesson is on <h1> headings, use <h1> tags. But have some fun with the heading you put inside the tags. Something like:

<h1>I'm Writing HTML! I Rule!</h1>

SEO, real sites: Your visitor might be Google's web crawler, looking to index your site for inclusion in search results. Google has taught its crawler that words inside <h1> headings are very important. That means they are

VERY IMPORTANT! Make sure any keyword terms or phrases are included in your headings, especially your `<h1>` headings.

`<p>`**Paragraphs in paragraph tags.**`</p>`

Time to write a poem! Enter something like this into your page:

```
Hear we are learning
HTML.
We'll master the skill,
And it will serve us well.
```

Try it!

> Online: Online: Knowits > HTML I > Online > 1 > 1c

When you view your page at this point, your browsers stretch that poem out in a single line (maybe two if it doesn't fit in one). This is not at all what you want. Suppose you had done better than our doggerel. Maybe you started:

```
Whose woods these are I think I know.
```

Well, you certainly wouldn't want that line ruined, would you? (Robert Frost, "Stopping by Woods on a Snowy Evening").

What is happening here is that the browser is taking the liberty of formatting your words to suit the available space. It assumes that text will fill the width available. So it unwraps your poem. Browsers are smart enough, however, to leave blank lines between paragraphs. Try the improvements shown here:

With that improvement, you see two lines, as if you had written two prose paragraphs. This is closer to what you want. Be patient: we'll get it exactly right, soon enough.

Unordered Lists

Now, a bit of HTML terminology. We have three kinds of lists that we can specify:

- Unordered (bullet) lists
- Ordered (numbered) lists
- Definition lists

We'll get all three. For now, we'll use the unordered (bullet) list, such as the one above. It takes two different block tags: `<ul>` and `<li>`. Both come with start and end tags. They stand for "unordered list" and "list item," respectively. The list above, in HTML, would be created this way:

```
<ul>
    <li>Unordered (bullet) lists</li>
    <li>Ordered (numbered) lists</li>
    <li>Definition lists</li>
</ul>
```

This is our first example of nested tags. The `<ul>...</ul>` pair surrounds `<li>...</li>` pairs.

Ready to try your own? For the next example, think of a short list of things you like: pizza toppings, musical instruments, friends… Think of things you like and follow our example, but use your own list.

Inline

A block, such as the four we've just covered, spans the full width of its container. Until you get advanced, its container is the page. If its content doesn't fit, it will cover as many lines as it needs. A new block will start below a preceding block. Inline content, by contrast, will run across the page, each new inline item will come to the right of the previous inline item until a line is filled. It will wrap to the next line when more space is needed.

These are directions for most western languages, of course. Our friends writing languages from the area in and near the Arabian peninsula—such as Arabic, Hebrew, Urdu and Persian—will be happy to know that their languages default to the reverse, right-to-left, direction. HTML also serves those who write the Asian languages that use word symbols often written from top-to-bottom. We will, however, focus on the western languages.

Inserting Breaks with `<br>`

Suppose you just want to break a line, but don't want to separate it into paragraphs. You use the `<br>` tag. Here's the final version of our poem:

Online: Knowits > HTML I > Online > 1 > 1f

When you try that last improvement, you have what you wanted: a poem!

Do Not Use the `<font>` Tag

Now we will introduce a tag you should not use. Bear with us. This will make sense.

As HTML has progressed, some original tags are "deprecated." This means that their continued use is not recommended by the W3C standards body. Deprecated tags may be dropped from future versions of HTML. A particularly important change in recent years has been the introduction of CSS, the Cascading Style Sheets markup sub language. With CSS, the advice has become to use HTML for "semantic" markup and to use CSS for "presentational" markup.

The word "semantic" refers to the concept "meaning." What does the language mean? Presentational markup specifies what the finished page should look like. WWW pages have a wide potential audience, and that audience includes visually impaired users who may not be able to see your page. For these users there are browsers that read web pages, others that present pages in braille and so on. Your presentational markup will be invisible to these people.

Are you going to go to extra trouble for these users? We hope so. For one reason, although the visually impaired are a small minority (beware of statistics to the contrary) there is almost no extra work required to support their special browsers. You just have to use CSS for your presentational markup. (The CSS alternatives to the `<font>` tag, for example, are far more capable. You'll want to use them if you can.)

SEO: And to be completely selfish, think about SEO. Remember that the Google web crawler, which will or won't include your site in search results, is not just "visually impaired," it's completely blind! If you want visitors to come to your site you will be sure to make your site as accessible as possible to the visually impaired.

That said, there are two perfectly good reasons for using deprecated, presentational HTML tags. One is that you are making a site for your youth soccer team, an audience that is all fully sighted. By its nature, your site has no meaning to a wider audience. The second is that you are learning HTML. While you intend to get to CSS in due course, for now you want an interim way to display things on the web. For you, we introduce the deprecated `<font>` tag.

The `<font>` tag has three attributes, without which it is meaningless. An "attribute" of a tag is a named value, included within the tag. Suppose you wanted to have some text in a larger size. You could do that this way:

```
Make this <font size='+2'>text
larger</font>.
```

These are the three font attributes:

- `<font color='xxx' …>`
- `<font face='xxx' ... >`
- `<font size='xxx' … >`

(You can use as many attributes as you like. Want a large, blue font? Try `<font size='+2' color='blue'>` big, blue text here `</font>`.)

The color may be a number from 1 (smallest) through 7 (largest). The default size is 3. The size may also be a digit prefixed by a "+" or "-" sign to increase/decrease the size. The face may be a font family, like Arial or Helvetica, or a pseudo family, like "serif" or "monospace." For serious design typography use CSS; for HTML use one of "monospace" or "sans-serif". Color may be an HTML color specification. For font colors, stick to names like "red", "blue" and "black". We exit sites that use white text on dark backgrounds, as fast as possible.

Remember that serif fonts, such as this text, are most readable in print. Sans-serif fonts are more readable on computer screens. The serifs are those little squiggles that decorate the letter ends:

- ## serifs on 'g's and 'G's
- ## sans-serif 'g's and 'G's

With that said, take a look at our next example. We have some fun with our "poem." Have some fun with yours, too.

Online: Knowits > HTML I > Online > 1 > 1g

To do this work (you really don't want to do this with fonts, but we will teach you the technique) make one change at a time. Edit, then view. Edit, then view. Be sure you keep changing browsers while you do this. Now a word about fonts and typography.

Professional designers take college courses in typography. If that is not you, stick to the basics. The experts employed by the browser makers have chosen their most readable fonts (with one exception) for general use. Don't overrule them unless you know what you are doing.

The `<span>`...`</span>` tag pair establishes the generic inline page element. Like `<font>`s without attributes, it does nothing by itself. The online material shows several examples of `<span>`s combined with just a wee bit of CSS, to give you the general idea. No need for you to use `<span>`s yet. This is just FYI.

If you really like serif fonts (such as the one you are reading right now) use "Times New Roman" in lieu of the generic "serif" font family. (MSIE chooses a truly horrible serif font by default.)

Online: Knowits > HTML I > Online > 1 > 1h

Project—Pick a Topic

This knowit is organized around your project, which gives you both a lot of freedom and a lot of responsibility. For starters, take a look at our sample:

Online: Knowits > HTML I > Project

Your assignment for this chapter is to pick a similar topic for your own project. Be sure you include a class of similar things (people are good), a geographic dispersion and a time component. These let you do an image map (such as our map of Europe where you can click on a scientist) and a time line (that will teach you all about HTML tables).

If you can research your project in Wikipedia you will have a ready source of images that are available for your use without danger of a nasty-gram from an irate attorney asking for damages for your copyright infringement. You are far safer covering historical figures than using living people.

Np++ Secrets—Handling Tabs

While you can generally just use Notepad++ as you would any other text editor, it has lots of features that make programming easier. Many of them are hiding right in plain sight. We'll point out at least one in each chapter.

Many are best tried online, including the tab handling. (It depends on little symbols that would be very hard to show in print.) So follow this drilldown and try it for yourself.

Online: Engineers > Frontend Tools > Notepad++ > More Np++ > Tabs

Character Entities

A standard keyboard can produce fewer than 100 characters by typing a key or pressing Shift and typing a key. An original IBM PC expanded the "alphabet" of symbols to a full 256 possibilities. (That's a full byte: eight consecutive bits.) This wasn't enough. We expanded again from one to two bytes per character, and HTML now has 64,000 possibilities, of which about 4,000 are regularly used.

So how do you get to all these characters without a keyboard the size of a soccer pitch? (That's roughly the size of an American football field, end zones included.) Character entities.

You can use numbers, both decimal and hexadecimal or, for a smaller but handier selection, you can use named character entities. We'll start with three that flag intellectual property for its owners (who may be particular about the uses of their property). These are:

- Copyright: ©
- Trademark: ™
- Registered Trademark: ®

Return to the chapter's Companion page for examples:

Online: Knowits > HTML I > Online > 1

A named character entity starts with an ampersand, "&", then has a name and ends with a semicolon, ";". Enter these into any handy web page to learn how to use them, to see them on a web page and to help you remember them.

Quiz

Choose the word or phrase that best completes each sentence.

1) SEO is critical to
    a) optimize searching speed.
    b) use Google effectively.
    c) attract visitors to your site.

2) The most important browser for website development is
    a) Firefox.
    b) Microsoft Internet Explorer.
    c) Google Chrome.
    d) All of the above.

3) The two parts of most web pages are
    a) head and body.
    b) tags and attributes.
    c) doctype and language.

4) The `<p>` tag is
    a) a part separator.
    b) used for parenthetical remarks.
    c) for paragraphs.

5) The `<ul>` tag is
    a) an inline tag.
    b) a block tag.
    c) an inline tag with attributes.
    d) a block tag around `<li>` tags.

6) The `<font>` tag is
    a) used for all wisdom.
    b) a modern styling device.
    c) deprecated.

7) Recommended font styles and families include
    a) Times, Helvetica, and Courier.
    b) Times New Roman, monospace, and sans-serif.
    c) Times Roman, Arial, and Bookman.

8) The default starting page is
    a) `home.html`.
    b) `index.html`.
    c) `start.html`.

9) The `<br>` tag
    a) has no closing tag.
    b) must always be properly closed.
    c) requires attributes.

10) Character entities have
    a) names and octal numbers.
    b) octal and decimal numbers.
    c) names and binary numbers.
    d) names, decimal and hexadecimal numbers.

2 Looking Good

In this chapter we're going to start creating professional web pages. We'll start a template, from which you can start all your other web pages and your project's home page. Time to open the Companion page:

Online: Knowits > HTML I > Online > 2

Before we get started, let's roll our history forward toward the age of computers.

History—Before Computers

The last megayear (of about 15,000 since the Big Bang—see "History" in Chapter 1) leads us to the age of electricity.

The ancient Egyptians knew that some fish defended themselves by giving electric jolts. Static charges were always present for those who pet even the gentlest cat. One 18th century tinkerer, with more curiosity than common sense, flew a kite in a storm, demonstrating that those great flashes called lightning were, in fact, electric. We would finally learn the relationship between electricity and magnetism, which led quickly to the electric motor. (Franklin's was impractical. Faraday's was better.)

The age of electricity really got rolling when Thomas Edison started to find interesting uses, such as illumination, phonographs and moving pictures. (Our French friends are saying, "but Lumiere was first with electric light!" True, but in engineering, getting things to actually work—and that means work at an affordable cost—counts for a lot.) "What good is this electricity?" Edison was asked. He answered, "What good is a baby?" (Or was that Franklin, paraphrased by Faraday?)

We already had telegraphy and then telephony. We would get radios that could actually pull music right out of thin air! Vacuum tubes let a very small signal (like a needle in a phonograph) modulate a very large signal (like one driving a speaker). And then Turing figured out how we might use these tubes to actually perform computations and the computer was born. Schockley's team at Bell Labs figured out how to replace the vacuum tube with transistors and we were off to the races.

If we measured the last megayear of mankind in units of about three human generations (66 years, which we could call *grandpayears*), again we'd have 14,999 out of 15,000 gone. The last grandpa year gets very interesting!

Clickable links on your Companion page: a brilliant note re Ben Franklin and the IEEE official history of electricity.

Websites—Design

Our histories are about to slow down. Our website building is about to speed up. In Chapter 1 we looked at SEO, because building a website with no visitors is a waste of time. Here we'll back up to the beginning and look at the design of your project website.

Many books have been written on website design. The ability to design a good-looking website is a wonderful skill, and one that is not easy to master. You won't learn it here.

If your budget permits, hire a designer! If your budget doesn't have a fat item for website design, you'll have to do it yourself. So here we present a few pointers.

Begin with another look at our sample project:

Online: Knowits > HTML I > Project

Note that every page looks a bit like every other page. They all share the same background color. They all have the same navigation bar at the top. The title and the double lines that separate navigation from title from page are all the same.

You want to choose some design elements for your site that are also all the same. And you don't want to labor over your choices at this point. You can change your mind as you get more into your project. (In fact, we'll show you how to use

Notepad++ to edit every page in your site with a single replace command.)

Design software can be frightfully expensive. Alternatively, you can grab a few sheets of white paper from your printer and some felt-tip markers. (Few designers work in HTML. It's too slow.) Steal some crayons from your baby sister, if that's all you can find. Start designing.

Begin with navigation. A simple list of pages, such as we have chosen, is easy to implement in HTML, and it's easy for a visitor to understand. We'll get into this more deeply in Chapter 4. For now, keep it simple and keep it consistent. Navigation, for left-to-right reading languages, should be either at the top or down the left side. Going down the left side requires CSS. For HTML, stick to the top.

Page color? You can leave it unspecified. Your visitors have either left their browsers to show basic white, or have chosen their own colors. Choosing a site-specific color helps to tie your pages together, but don't stray too far from white.

Graphics? We hope your topic comes with a natural set of images, such as the portraits we've used for our scientists. Their painters all seemed partial to brown backgrounds, (which we thought about when we chose a page color).

Typefaces? Use "sans-serif" for your entire site and use "Times New Roman" for headings, just for variety. (We chose "Times New Roman" for the main text. It's not as easy to read online, but we didn't have a lot of reading material in the site. It seemed appropriate for the 17th century topic.) Ignore this advice if you are a designer who knows typography. For really enjoying the design of websites, books and even TV shows, your life will be richer if you learn a little bit about typography. But that's not this book's subject.

Now think about decorative elements. Keep them simple. A double-line rule between sections is all you'll really need if your material has a nice mix of print and images.

Finally, avoid the temptation to center things. The very worst designs on the web are the ones with everything centered.

Tools—Opera

Why Opera? As a browser it has a tiny market share. We do almost nothing in Opera that's different from what we do in important browsers, such as Chrome and Firefox. There aren't many Opera-specific "gotchas" (and the few we've found are deep into the wonders of JavaScript programs, not HTML).

So why Opera? The Error Console.

HTML is very forgiving. If you make a mistake, browsers will simply ignore the mistake. (You meant to type `<h1>` but your right hand wasn't paying attention so you got `<j1>`.) You'd notice that your heading wasn't heading-sized, perhaps, and look to find the trouble, but your browsers wouldn't say anything about it.

So turn on the Opera Error Console. If you leave just a couple centimeters showing to the left of Opera, you'll see when it reports any problem. One click gives you an explanation. (Mostly, it's just a simple typo. Tell your hands to pay attention!)

To turn it on, see the Chapter 2 Companion page. It has a big color picture. The keyboard shortcut is Ctrl+Shift+O. (We're not big fans of complex "shortcuts" but this one we know well.)

Head—Commented Template

In this chapter's "Head" section we'll cover comments, notes to yourself, and the three basic blocks tags of almost every HTML page.

Comments to Yourself

A comment is a note to yourself. The text marked as a comment is read by the computer only to find where it ends, after which the computer will get back to its business. You, on the other hand, are vitally interested in the comments because, after all, you took the time to write them. (If your work is inherited by someone else, the comments become that much more important. "What," he or she asks, "is going on here?")

A comment is formed this way:

```
<!-- this is an HTML comment -->
```

The comment is commonly put on a line by itself. It may span multiple lines, or it may be on a line with your HTML content, too. The important thing is the start and end characters.

We always start our pages (just after the doctype) with a comment that tells you the file path and name, along with a few words describing the page. We end (at the very end) with a comment that tells you this is the end of the page:

```
<!DOCTYPE html>

<!-- folder/foo.html - page describing
"foo" -->


. . . page content here

<!-- end of foo.html -->
```

The Companion page link will tell you more, if you really want to know.

Now on to tags. One of them is actually the <head> tag.

The <html> Tag

In Chapter 1 we entered and viewed HTML without the <html> tag. (And with no <head> nor <body> tags, either.) How did that work?

If you omit these tags, the browsers assume you are entering HTML in the <body> section. You can omit these tags, but if you omit them, HTML checkers, such as the W3C Validator we'll use in Chapter 7, will be annoyed. Putting these tags into a template, that we'll get to momentarily, gets them into your pages with no extra effort at all.

The <html> tag should start, and the </html> tag should end every HTML page, excepting only the doctype and comments.

The <head> Tag

If you want to have head-section material in your HTML page (and you definitely will want this) it must come between `<head>` and `</head>` tags. Omit these and you will not have a head section and any head section tags will be ignored.

The `<body>` Tag

The body section comes between `<body>` and `</body>` tags. Including them is necessary if you want to validate your pages.

The Page Template

You'll see how these tags work together when you make your page template, per the directions at:

Online: Knowits > HTML I > Online > 2 > 2a

Save your `template.html` file where it will be handy, but not too handy. (It is very easy to ruin a template by typing page-specific HTML into a generic template where it will be totally wrong, the next time you want to use the template). And then save your template in another place, where it will be available if you (when you?) inadvertently ruin the original.

Blocks—`<h2>` through `<h6>`

As you may have guessed, there are more headings than just `<h1>`. There are six, in total. As a practical matter, the first three or four have uses as headings in web pages. The last two, `<h5>` and `<h6>`, are only useful in places such as the fine print of legal documents. `<h4>` is very close to the size of regular text, though often emphasized (as with bold or italic attributes).

The second example shows you how to build your own menu of headings, so you can see for yourself. It is also the first example to use your new template file. Instructions are online.

Online: Knowits > HTML I > Online > 2 > 2b

Inline—Mono and Global

We'll cover two topics in this section. First, we'll look at all the inline elements that use monospaced fonts.

Monospaced font elements are used for showing program code (for example, the file listings in the online pages). And they are used for showing old-fashioned keyboard input, screen samples and variable names. (If you guess that HTML was originally used to talk about computers and computer programs you are absolutely right.) Will you ever use these? It depends on your subjects.

Then we'll move on to the universal (or global) attributes that can be used with every tag, block or inline.

Monospaced Font Tags

There are four monospaced font tags available. They are:

- `<code>` such as for code listings
- `<kbd>` for showing typed (keyboard) input
- `<samp>` for computer output samples
- `<var>` possibly for variable names

We'll show these in example 2c and move right along. If you can surround headings with heading tags, you can surround monospaced elements with any of these tags.

Universal (or Global) Tag Attributes

You've seen `<font>` attributes such as `size` and `color`. Some attributes are called "universal" in HTML 4 and "global" in HTML5. Both mean the same thing: you can use them with any tag in HTML.

Neither "universal" nor "global" should be taken too literally. Some tags are quite unsuited for some attributes. (What color is a `<br>`? Perhaps the same color as one hand clapping?)

The attributes are used with any tags where they make even a little sense. However, we haven't discussed HTML 4 and HTML 5 standards yet. Our histories will treat them fully, but we're not there. For the moment, HTML 4 is the current standard HTML. It's been with us since 1999. HTML 5 is the coming standard. It's due to be made final in 2014. (It is less common for a standard to be finalized on time than for one to be years late. We'll see.) In the meantime, we have taken the attributes that are both universal in HTML 4 and global in HTML 5 as the set that you should know about and use today.

The dual-standard universal/global attributes are:

- class
- dir
- lang
- style
- title

The dir attribute refers to language direction. If you will be using Arabic and Hebrew (or other Semitic languages), you will need to look into this on your own.

The style attribute lets you use CSS styles on individual elements. This jumps ahead to Volume 2 of this series. For a taste, the following would make a paragraph's background red:

```
<p style='background-color: red'>This would be red!</p>
```

The class attribute is also CSS-dependent. You would use it when you wanted a certain class of paragraphs to all be red, for instance.

Last, and most immediately helpful, the title attribute lets you assign a title to an element. When the user hovers the mouse over an element with a title, the title is shown as a tooltip.

The online example shows monospaced elements with tooltips:

Online: Knowits > HTML I > Online > 2 > 2c

Project—Create Your Site

Now that you have a template, you can create the first page of your website. The first page is called `index.html`. In a browser, if you ask for "google.com" in the address bar, your browsers see that the address (more exactly, the URL —Uniform Resource Locator) has no page specified. So it adds `index.html` for you. (The browser also sees that your address has no "transfer protocol" so it adds the default— http for HyperText Transfer Protocol—for you and navigates to "`http://MartinRinehart.com/index.html`").

You'll need the page name for now. Remember that home pages are called `index.html`. You'll need the transfer protocol when you start creating links to external pages. We'll remind you when we get there.

You'll also need a folder. Something like "english-lady-novelists" would be good (assuming, of course, that your project is about English lady novelists). This is a time for a word on folder and file names.

The Windows operating systems are "case-insensitive" for folder and file names. All of these are pathnames for the same Windows file:

- `foo/bar.html`
- `Foo/Bar.html`
- `foo/Bar.HTML`

In Unix-derived operating systems (including Linux and Apple's OS/X) those names are all different. Folders `foo` and `Foo` are different, separate folders. Files `bar.html` and `Bar.HTML` are different, separate files. Why do you care?

You care because you will develop on your local system (likely Windows) and then upload your finished website to an Internet Service Provider (ISP) when it is ready for the world at large. Your ISP will probably use Linux-based servers. Differences in case in the folder and file names that were hidden when you built your system suddenly are broken links (and, as Murphy's Law would predict, at the worst possible moment: just when you are ready to go live).

What do you do? The simple, foolproof solution is to never, ever use a capital letter in a folder or file name. There are similar "gotcha"s in multi-word names. We always separate our multi-word names with hyphens, not underscores or spaces, and recommend that you do, too.

Now, let's build that starting page. (Remember that when you look at our examples, they are all for our sample project. Your names should all be different, of course.) Start by making your folder. Then open your template and immediately save it as `index.html` in your new folder.

Add a major heading and you are done.

Online: Knowits > HTML I > Online > 2 > 2d

If you are smart, you will use the blank space to make notes to yourself about the pages you plan to add and whatever else comes to mind.

That was easy, wasn't it? This project work will be much easier than you might have guessed. In fact, so will HTML!

Np++ Secrets—Vertical Space

Vertical space is a precious commodity if you create web content. Except in the very early stages of a project, your editor isn't tall enough to show your complete pages. This is odd.

The history of computers is full of constraints that have stopped being constraining. In the old days, computer memory was fantastically expensive and therefore scarce. Today a gigabyte of extra memory costs little more than a first-class sandwich. Disk space? It's nearly free if you don't make a habit of storing full-length movies on your hard drive.

But vertical space is still a limited, expensive commodity. Notepad++ can help, but only a little. So do check the following page, and do take its advice regarding the main menu (even if it scares you!).

Online: Engineers > Frontend Tools > Notepad++ > Lines

Entities—Accents

The World-wide Web was originally based on U.S. Standards, such as ASCII: the American Standard Code for Information Interchange. The original ASCII used some control characters (linefeed, return and so forth), 26 letters (A through Z, uppercase only), digits zero through nine and some punctuation marks. All of these could be represented in just six bits. As communications lines were fabulously expensive, six-bit letters were chosen over 7-bit letters. (Seven bits would have permitted lowercase letters, too).

Official use of 8-character alphabets didn't take over the Web until 2007. Today's web is based on 16-character "letters" which allow for encoding most modern languages, including Asian ones (based on full-word symbols) as well as many now extinct languages important to scholars who study the development of written language.

In past years, and still today, character entities filled in the gaps for western languages with a simple, elegant system that permits a variety of accents that let you write, more or less correctly, most of the languages in use in Europe and the Americas. This is described on the Companion page for Chapter 2.

Online: Knowits > HTML I > Online > 2

Though we're not big fans of memorizing facts (in an era when "google" has become a verb—why memorize when you can google it?) but knowing some character entities is very handy. So these will be on the quiz (where you can still google the answers, but it will take you a little longer).

Quiz

Choose the word or phrase that best completes each sentence.

1) An inventor, asked about the value of electricity, answered, "What good is a baby?" His name was
    a) Edison.
    b) Lumiere.
    c) Franklin.
    d) Farady.

2) Website design is
    a) an art best done by professional designers.
    b) worst when everything is centered.
    c) concerned with site navigation.
    d) all of the above.

3) The best font families for non-typographers are
    a) Arial and Helvetica.
    b) Times Roman and other traditional fonts.
    c) serif, sans-serif and monospace.
    d) Bookman and Vera Sans.

4) Three page structuring tags are
    a) `<html>`, `<doctype>` and `<body>`.
    b) `<header>`, `<body>` and `<footer>`.
    c) `<html>`, `<head>` and `<body>`.
    d) `<doctype>`, `<head>` and `<foot>`.

5) Heading tags `<h5>` and `<h6>` are
    a) used for mid-sized headings.
    b) used after the first four headings.
    c) too small for common use.

6) The home page is commonly named
- a) `home page.`
- b) `home.html.`
- c) `index.html.`
- d) `home-page.html.`

7) Folder and file names are
- a) not case-sensitive.
- b) case-sensitive.
- c) never used in lowercase.
- d) best in all lowercase.

8) Websites are most commonly served by
- a) Windows computers.
- b) Apple computers.
- c) Linux computers.

9) Modern HTML uses up to
- a) 6-bit characters.
- b) 7-bit characters.
- c) 8-bit characters.
- d) 16-bit characters.

10) Character entity accent names include
- a) acute, circumflex and tilde.
- b) grave, tilde and umlaut.
- c) acute, grave and umlaut.
- d) acute, tilde and uml.

3 Populate Your Pages

There are lots of important milestones in this chapter. To begin, our history will get to the birth of the Internet, an event as important as any in the last century. Then we'll plan the pages in our project website. Ready to use Latin in your developing pages? (Faux Latin, of course, and it's been used for centuries.) Ready to add colors and pictures (big things!) and footnotes (important things!) to your site?

Start online at the Companion page.

Online: Knowits > HTML I > Chapters > 3

Now, here comes the Internet.

History—Birth of the Internet

By the middle of the last century, we had huge mainframe computers and atomic bombs. A chief source of research funding was the U.S. government, which thought that U.S. security depended on these things. The Defense Advanced Research Project Agency (DARPA) wanted a way to interconnect the computers (that controlled the bombs). They wanted this to be so secure that it would withstand a nuclear attack on the U.S.

A technology called "packet switching" was invented that let each computer in a network function as a controller of the network. If one fails, the rest of the network can continue operating. This answered the essential defense problem.

On October 29, 1969, a student programmer sent the first message over the "ARPANET". It was the word "login". The network crashed after two characters. Later the same evening, the whole word was successfully sent and one computer logged in to another. By December 5, four separate computers were communicating over the ARPANET and the Internet was born. (We're not magic-driven numerologists, but that was about 15,000 days ago.)

http://www.pbs.org/opb/nerds2.0.1/geek_glossary /packet_switching_flash.html Packet switching

Websites—What Pages?

Website design only has a neat set of steps in theory. In practice, you have to do it almost all at once. You decide what it will look like and you decide what pages you have before you get started.

In this chapter you will add pages for all those you want. Right now, begin thinking about the pages you want. In our sample project, that is:

- home page
- time line
- map
- one page per scientist
- Newton's "quotes"
- credits

Your design should be similar. If you want your "quotes" all in "Latin" the next section will show you how we do it.

Tools—*Lorem Ipsum*

In the 1500s an unknown printer wrote these immortal words:

> *Lorem ipsum dolor sit amet, consectetur adipiscing elit. Ut quam arcu, sodales ac facilisis sed, tempus ac orci. In scelerisque ultrices fermentum. Curabitur quis mi ligula.*

What do they mean? Absolutely nothing. The printer was soliciting business. He wanted to show potential clients what their documents might look like. He'd seen some work by Cicero and he invented a way of dropping in letters that would look like Latin. Ever since, "Lorem ipsum" (the first two words of his classic text) has been used to demonstrate the look of the page, without the distraction of having real text.

Where do you get Lorem Ipsum? You google. Sites like `lipsum.com` (clickable link on Companion page) have generators for you. Most are free.

Here you have one of the least likely distinctions between professional and amateur HTML Professionals know where to go to get their nonsense.

Head—`<style>`, `<script>`

This chapter's lesson on the head section will be brief.

You will see pages that interest you, not for their content but for their HTML. You will right-click the page in your browser and it will give you an option to "View Source" (or "View Page Source" or just "Source"). You will look at the page's HTML. Near the top, you'll see the head section.

In addition to head-specific tags (page author, keywords and so on) you may see a `<style>` section in the `<head>` section.

The `<style>` section is where you will see any page-specific CSS. (Larger websites will have most of the CSS in separate CSS files. Those can be applied to multiple pages or even the whole site.) The `<style>` section ends with an `</style>` tag, as you might have guessed. We hope this encourages you to go on to Volume 2 in this series. It's all about CSS.

Many pages also have `<script>` sections in the head, also ended by `</script>` tags. This is for JavaScript program code. Today it is not considered best practice to put JavaScript in the head. (Putting it at the end of the body is preferred.) But you will see it there in older pages, and in pages where the author isn't aware of current best practices. We hope the `<script>` encourages you to go on to Volume 3!

In the Companion page, we show these tags added to the template.

Blocks—Colors, `<ol>`s

Now we dive into the content of the body section, beginning with block elements. In this chapter, we'll concentrate on the attributes that add color to blocks.

Today, CSS is recommended for color. Color is, of course, presentational, not semantic. It is used to get the appearance you want, such as a page color. Of course, you might use the color red to highlight warnings, which would be semantic. (If you do so, remember that some people cannot see the color. Use words, too.)

The `bgcolor` Attribute

Prior to CSS, color was specified in the `bgcolor` (think "background color") attribute of blocks. Let's get to examples momentarily.

The `bgcolor` attribute was deprecated in HTML 4 and dropped entirely from HTML 5. We definitely recommend using CSS, instead. However, if CSS is in your future while HTML is in your present, don't be afraid to use `bgcolor`. We guess that all browsers will still support it for many years.

Use `bgcolor` with `<body>` and `<table>` Blocks

Would you like a nice light brown, parchment feel for your pages? In the `<body>` section, try:

```
<body bgcolor='#f8f4f0'>
```

(Don't fret over `f8f4f0`. It specifies a color and we'll explain how, below.) It's usual to think of blocks as elements you use in the body section. However, the body section is, itself, a block.

Would you like a nice light blue background for a table? Try:

```
<table bgcolor='#f0f0ff'>
```

We'll get to tables in Chapter 5. For now, remember that you can use the `bgcolor` attribute with tables, individual table rows and single cells within rows.

Specific Colors

Now, how do you specify a color? You use names (like 'blue') or hexadecimal numbers. We're pretty sure you're familiar with decimal numbers; we'll explain hexadecimal numbers ("hex" for short). But first a word about computer colors.

Most computer displays use RGB colors. That stands for red, green and blue. A standard desktop monitor uses only these three colors, each in intensity varying from zero (off) through 255 (maximum on). Black is no color: R, G and B all turned off. White is all on: R, G and B guns all on maximum.

We use the names "white" and "black" as a shorthand for "all on" and "all off." Otherwise, color names are nearly useless. Primary colors, "red" and "blue," mean what they say: "red" is, for example, 100% red, no green and no blue. The name "green" stands for a green color, but not pure green. As colors, the primaries are suitable for decorating kids blocks, but not much else.

And that brings us to hexadecimal numbers. Decimal numbers use a "base" of ten, represented with digits as "10". (Say that to yourself not as "ten" but as "one, zero".)

Two digit decimal numbers are one of `00, 01, 02, …
98, 99`.

Hexadecimal numbers use a base of sixteen, also represented with digits as "10" (again, "one, zero"). For single digits, hex numbers use the familiar "0" through "9" (zero through nine) followed by "a" through "f" (ten through fifteen). Hex is very convenient with computers which internally handle data as bytes: 8-bit chunks. In hex a byte is one of `00, 01, 02, … fe, ff`.

The hex numbering assigns two digits to each of the primary colors, preceded by a "#": `#rrggbb`. The first two hex digits specify the amount of red. "`00`" means no red at all. "`ff`" means 255, the maximum. Ditto for the green and blue colors.

If you don't worry about numbers you'll be happy choosing your colors. It's like mixing paint out of the can. You pour a bit of blue into the white and stir. Too light? You pour in a bit more blue. Unlike mixing paint you do not need to wear old clothes. Most important, if you get a bit too much blue it's easy to take some out. (That's in HTML. It's not so easy with old-fashioned paint.)

Another very important difference between computer and paint colors is that adding dark colored paints gives you, if they're dark enough, a near-black. Computer colors are the reverse: add equal parts r, g and b and you get gray. Add more of each and you get a lighter gray. Add the maximum of each and you get white. The Companion page encourages you to experiment:

Online: Knowits > HTML I > Online > 3

At the risk of repeating, we'll say again: experiment.

But don't obsess! Some designers hang expensive color meters on their monitors. This made more sense designing for print than it does today. Today you could get the exact shade you wanted, only to find that it doesn't come out the same way in all browsers. Then you find that it's not the same on all monitors. And then you notice that colors change, and change a lot!, as you view your laptop from different angles. Have fun with colors, but don't obsess.

Ordered Lists

Ordered lists, with one small addition, are just as simple as unordered lists. You just change `<ul>` ... `</ul>` to `<ol>` ... `</ol>` and your bullet list is now a "numbered" list. Now for that one small addition.

Unordered lists, as you recall, have a type attribute that can be one of:

- `type='circle'`
- `type='disc'`
- `type='square'`

Here's a simple, ordered list:

1. try an ordered list
2. try the type attribute
3. make an outline

By default, an ordered list is numbered. Numbered with simple, old-fashioned Arabic numerals. Now for the type attribute. It can be one of the following:

- `type='I'`
- `type='A'`
- `type= '1'`
- `type='i'`
- `type='a'`

Yes, those are the "numbering" styles you use with an outline. Your Companion page has samples:

Online: Knowits > HTML I > Online > 3

Inline—Images

The National Center for Supercomputing Applications (NCSA, University of Illinois at Urbana-Champaign) released the Mosaic browser in 1993.It took the world by storm because it supported pictures. Until then, the World-Wide Web had been a text-only system. 1993 changed it forever. (Lead programmer Marc Andreesen, along with investor Jim Clark, went on to found Netscape and become the Internet's first mega-rich.)

Today, images are very simple. You just drop in an `<img>` tag, a few attributes and you have done what was, just 20 years ago an amazing feat.

The `<img>` tag has no closing tag. You don't put your picture into the HTML. You put your picture's address in the `src` attribute. Here's an example:

```
<img
    alt='Picture of my puppy.'
    border=0
    src='graphics/my_puppy.png'
    title='Picture of my puppy.'
>
```

(You could put the tag and its attributes all on a single line, if you want. HTML doesn't care. We like this format because it's easy for us to read, not because any browsers care.)

The `alt` attribute is the 'alternate' that will be read or otherwise used by browsers for the visually impaired. SEO! Remember that the `alt` attribute is the only way a web crawler can find out about what is in a picture.

Microsoft's browsers put a one-pixel border around images, by default. All other browsers default to no border. Most people do not want the browsers adding borders, but you have to specify `border=0` to keep MSIE from adding a border. Alternatively, you would have to add `border=1` if you wanted browsers to add a one-pixel border. This is so annoying!

The `src` attribute is the one that tells the browser where to go to get the picture. Many put pictures into a subfolder called "graphics," as assumed here. If your page is in `whatever/folder/page.html`, then the sample picture would be found in `whatever/folder/graphics/my_puppy.png`.

Last, we come to the tooltip. Some browsers will use the `alt` attribute for a tooltip, if you don't provide a `title`. Some won't. If you include the `title` attribute, it will be used by all browsers as the tooltip. If you don't want a tooltip, use `title=''`.

Note that the slashes between folder, subfolder and file names go forward, Unix style, not backward, Windows style. Note also that there is no slash before the folder name in `src='subfolder/filename.xxx'`.

What kind of picture files? All common ones work well: `.gif`, `.png`, `.jpg` (aka `.jpeg`). Some less common ones also work well: `.tiff`, `.raw`, `.bmp`. Chances are that if you downloaded a file from the web or uploaded a file from your camera you can use it.

What size? The picture on your site will be whatever size the picture is in the file unless you specify the `height` and/or `width` attributes of the `<img>` tag. (If you specify one, not the other, the browser will maintain the original aspect ratio. If you specify both you can distort the picture.) It used to be a bad practice to use the browser to resize the picture (it was better to resize in expensive software like Photoshop). Today's browsers can resize quite nicely. Of course, if you start with a very small picture and display it at a very large size, it will be fuzzy. Browsers don't work miracles.

Project—Your Pages

Here we'll create a starting page for each of the pages in your project website.

First, create a list of your pages. Give them readable names. `jane-austen.html` would be good for a page about Jane Austen.

Second, open your `index.html`. Save As … your second project page. (Your first is `index.html`, of course.) Now change the heading to correctly name your page. Repeat, but not before you read the next paragraph.

When you come to the people that will populate your site (or trees, or frogs or …) add an `<img>` for the photo or painting that illustrates that person. Write a sentence or two about each person. Or grab a little Lorem Ipsum. Visit our sample project, any scientist and right-click View Source if you have any question about how it's done.

Now, make one page for each of your project's final pages. Add images as appropriate. You now have the makings of a website. Or at least you would have if there were some way to navigate from page to page. We'll get there, next chapter.

Npp Secrets—Sessions

A programmer's editor must, (not should, must!) store exactly what you type in its file. Anything else would probably be disastrous.

But Notepad++ may know more. The first, obvious thing is your position at the top, bottom or somewhere in the middle of the file. If you want Notepad++ to remember the extras, but not add anything to your HTML, you should know about its Sessions. If you want to have exactly three pages open for one part of your project, but have four other pages open for something else, you definitely want to know about Sessions.

Online: Engineers > Frontend Tools > Notepad++ > Sessions

Entities—Three Footnotes

HTML lets you go as far as you like with footnotes. But if your needs are simple and three footnotes are enough, there is nothing quicker than the superscript character entities.

If you want four or more footnotes, you can still use these for the first three.

Quiz

Choose the word or phrase that best completes each sentence.

1) The Internet developed from a perceived need to
   a) communicate via email.
   b) hyperlink documents.
   c) survive a nuclear attack.

2) Website designs begin with
   a) the "look" of the site.
   b) the "look and feel" of the site.
   c) the content of pages.
   d) all of the above.

3) "Lorem ipsum" is
   a) the start of a famous essay by Cicero.
   b) Latin from the 1500s.
   c) non-Latin from the 1500s.
   d) a university slogan.

4) When used
   a) `<script>` goes in the head, `<style>` in the body.
   b) `<script>` and `<style>` go in the body.
   c) `<script>` and `<style>` go in the head.
   d) `<style>` goes in the head, `<script>` at the end of the body.

5) The `bgcolor` attribute is
   a) deprecated in HTML 5.
   b) used for image backgrounds.
   c) introduced in HTML 4.
   d) still available but not recommended.

6) The `border` attribute of an image tag
    a) is required if you don't want borders.
    b) is required if you do want borders.
    c) is required if you care about borders.
    d) is required if you don't care about borders.

7) The color black may be specified as
    a) `'black'`.
    b) `'#000000'`.
    c) both of the above.
    d) neither of the above.

8) The `alt` attribute of the `<img>` tag
    a) provides information to the visually impaired.
    b) is read by search engine web crawlers.
    c) may be used as a tooltip.
    d) all of the above.

9) Footnotes may be shown by character entities
    a) if you use four or fewer.
    b) if you adopt MLA style footnotes.
    c) if you specify the original source.
    d) none of the above.

10) Mosaic was
    a) the first text-mode browser.
    b) programmed at the University of Michigan.
    c) programmed at Michigan State University.
    d) commercialized by Netscape.

4 Navigate (Obviously)

You will need to offer your visitor some way to navigate among your site's pages, obviously. But that "obvious" is a double entendre. The need for navigation is obvious and the navigation itself must be obvious. In this chapter you'll learn how to create links and use them to link your separate pages into a single site.

Time again to turn to the chapter Companion page:

Online: Knowits > HTML I > Online > 4

We begin with the birth of the World-Wide Web, which is not, as you'll see, a synonym for the Internet. It is an application of the Internet.

History—Birth of the WWW

The Internet, nee ARPANET, was born in 1969. Twenty years later it connected major universities around the world, governments (particularly military departments) and some large corporations. The first major application was electronic mail, which became common among those with Internet access. Just as electricity was a necessary technology before computers could be developed, the Internet was necessary before the World-Wide Web could be born.

The WWW was born in 1989. Its inventor was Tim (now Sir Tim) Berners-Lee, a young computer programmer working at CERN, the Swiss physics laboratory. He envisioned scientific papers in which footnotes were replaced by embedded links that gave the researcher access to the actual paper with a single mouse click. The collection of all such "hyperlinked" papers would combine to form the "World-Wide Web". (This idea first appeared as part of science-fiction by Arthur C. Clarke and earlier writers.)

Working with co-inventor Robert Cailliau, Berners-Lee turned his desktop microcomputer into the world's first web server and the world's first WWW client. Along the way fundamental problems were solved, such as creating a protocol for computers to use when sharing documents (HTTP—hypertext transfer protocol) and a language to "markup" documents so they could be shared: HTML, our HyperText Markup Language.

In 1989, computers with bitmap displays (and bitmap-capable printers) shared life alongside computers with older technology. One essential problem (solved by HTML) was that sharing papers meant sharing them with readers of widely different capabilities. (Today's better telephones have more computing power than the large computers of 1989. Today we wonder if our website's visitor has the Arial typeface or something better. Back then you might wonder if your reader's printer had upper- and lowercase letters.)

`http://www.zakon.org/robert/internet/timeline/`History of ARPANET

Websites—Navigation

The first website that went beyond one page was the first that needed to solve the navigation problem. If you have two pages, putting a "Next" link on one and a "Previous" link on the other will work. However, it won't work very well.

First, duplicating those links at the top and bottom of the page would be nice (unless your pages are very short). Second, if your reader has enjoyed the first two pages, s/he will probably be looking for the third. Putting a disabled "Next" link on the last page will do the job. Or you could use "First" and "Last" for your links.

If you have three or more pages these concerns are magnified. If the site is large you may need a trail showing where the viewer is located. "Breadcrumb" navigation (after the children in the fairy tale who dropped breadcrumbs in the forest so they could find their way home) is common:

Home > Sporting Goods > Boating > Kayaks > Paddles

The best navigation lets the visitors know where they are and lets them see how they might get to another location. And it makes this obvious.

Tools—Dictionaries

Ah, the good old days! The author was never without a dictionary. Should that be the abridged edition (handy, affordable, incomplete) or the unabridged (cumbersome, expensive, but it's got the answer)?

Let's google "definitions" and see what we find.

Using Google to google, before the start of the search results we have a definition: "a statement of the exact meaning ..." and we have links to Wikipedia, Answers.com, Merrian-Webster and The Free Dictionary.

The we get search results for dictionary.reference.com, definitions.net, en.wikipedia.org/wiki/Definition and ... What's this? A personal training studio named "Definitions"? Oh, yeah. Right. Muscular definition. Get ripped. That's the trouble with words and computers, isn't it?

The good news is that today you have lots of dictionaries, many unabridged, most free and all are much faster to use than even the old abridged versions. And they come with lots of examples.

Let's see, "double entendre." Do we put "entendre" in italics as a foreign word? (No. It's originally French, but now considered part of English, too.)

You do make a habit of typing "define: word-to-look-up" into the Google search box, don't you?

Head—`<title>`

You have the Companion page for Chapter 4 open in one of your browsers, right? In the tab (and maybe on the title bar, too) it says "FeE 1: HTML Companion 4," right? (Well, maybe it only says as much of that as space permits. Clicking maximize should get the rest, if you don't have too many tabs open.) How did we get that title into the tab and title bar?

Simple. We put it into the `<title>` element in the `<head>`. We always start out our `<head>` sections with a title, like this:

```
...<head><title>Page Title Goes Here</title>
```

There's really nothing to it. However, you'll want to title all your pages, and that means you'll want the title in your template. The cookbook with this recipe is in the Companion page. Follow carefully:

Online: Knowits > HTML I > Online > 4

SEO: Search engines rely heavily on your title. Make sure it includes the words your visitors might use when they search for you.

Now, on to two very simple block elements for the body section.

Blocks—More Blocks

Now we come to two blocks that are simple, but you should think before you use them. They are both presentational and deprecated. Neither, however, has an adequate substitute even in CSS, so we still feel free to use them. If your boss insists that you validate your HTML (with the W3C or other Validator, see Chapter 7, Tools—Validators), don't use them.

`<hr>`

The horizontal rule, `<hr>` has no closing tag. It stands alone. It's attributes are:

- `align`
- `noshade`
- `size`
- `width`

The `align` attribute's value can be one of `left`, `center` or `right`. The `noshade` attribute doesn't have any value except `noshade` (that's right, `<hr noshade='noshade'>`). This is positively silly but was mandatory in XHTML, which is becoming extinct because of things like this. The `size` attribute's value is a number of pixels, defaulting to one. The width value is a number of pixels, such as `'200px'`, or a percentage such as `'80%'` (default: `'100%'`). To draw a line under most of your page, try:

```
<hr align='center' width='80%'>
```

To be exact, the `<hr>` tag is not deprecated. All of its attributes were deprecated in HTML 4, and are not supported in HTML 5. You can style your horizontal rules with CSS (if you go on to learn CSS).

`<center>`

The `<center>` tag is deprecated in HTML 4, not supported in HTML 5. Unless your boss insists otherwise, go ahead and use it. CSS is great for styling, but mediocre (or worse) at layout. It has no better alternative for centering things.

We heartily disapprove of W3C's eagerness to deprecate features that have no replacements. (And it is highly unlikely that any browser will drop support for `<center>` in the foreseeable future. Use it this way:

```
<center>
        This text will be centered.
</center>
```

Of course, if you resist the temptation to center things, chances are your pages will be better designed. You just might want to swear off using `<center>` for that reason.

Nested Lists

Now, one small point that has quite important implications: lists can nest. So far we've used simple text for list items. In fact, you can tuck just about anything you like within `<li>` ... `</li>` tags. That includes other lists. Or paragraphs, pictures, tables, and almost anything else that an HTML page can contain. Your Companion page has an example:

Online: Knowits > HTML I > Online > 4 "Nested Lists"

Quoted Attributes

So far we've shown many of our attribute's values in quotes: `<hr width='80%'>`. Do you really need the quotes?

Sometimes. If an attribute value includes spaces, it really needs the quotes. If you want to validate your pages, the rules for whether quotes are required are more strict. (How strict? Don't quote any attribute values and see what your validator says.) Validators vary. Valid XHTML requires quotes (which is another reason people avoid it).

If you're adroit with the keyboard, the easy way is to just quote attributes. If you're not too good on the keyboard …

Single or double quotes? Single quotes (apostrophes, really) are easier to type. If you need to embed quotes, use the non-embedded ones on the outside: `"Don't go!"`, for example.

Inline—the `<a>` Tag

Here we'll introduce the `<a>` tag. (Would you have chosen `<a>` for links? The tag morphed. Imagine the human appendix one day deciding that being an appendix was not helpful, so it decided to become a spleen.)

If you are a "learn by doing" person, fear not. For our project, we'll add navigation built entirely of links. You'll get all the "doing" you want.

First, let's talk about the anchor (`<a>`) tag. As you'll see in Chapter 7, we still use `<a>` for intra-page anchors. To be technical, HTML 5 doesn't even require `<a>` for anchors, but we are too sentimental to just heave it overboard. Now lets talk about using it for links.

First, HTML5 links are no longer inline content (what HTML5 calls "phrasing"). They can be used as blocks (HTML5 "flow"), too. This means they are more flexible. Using them as just inline elements will, however, work in all browsers, including older ones such as MSIE 8.

A link has two main parts. It has an internal part that addresses the page to which you are linking. It's external part is what the user sees and will click. Roughly:

```
<a href='page-to-load-when-
clicked.html'> Link to… </a>
```

(Please don't use the word "click". It's inappropriate for touch screens; it's wrong for browsers for the visually impaired and it's pretty silly even for people clicking with their mice. They know that you click links.)

The part between the `<a>` tag and its closing `</a>` is the visible link. Make sure it says, "Jane Austen's mother" if it leads to a page about Jane Austen's mother. SEO: Do you think a web crawler is helped by the words "click here"? This is the part that will be shown in the user's default colors for unvisited, and then for visited, links. (You can change these colors. Don't do so unless you are trying to confuse your visitors. CSS gives you full control of unvisited and visited colors if confusion is your goal.)

The value of the `href` attribute is the address of the page to load. If the page is in the same folder as the one containing the current page, don't use folders in the address. Just provide the name.

When we were beginners, the business about folders regularly tripped us up. Even when we understood it completely, it still tripped us up. Here's the explanation. You are in folder "me", a subfolder of "mom". You have a subfolder named "baby." Here is the structure:

- `mom/moms-file.html`

- `mom/me/my-file.html`, also `mom/me/sibling-file.html`

- `mom/me/baby/baby-file.html`

Here is the navigation:

- me to sibling: `<a href='sibling-file.html'>`

- me to mom: `<a href='../moms-file.html'>`

- me to baby: `<a href='baby/baby-file.html'>`

If your link is failing your `href` and the actual address aren't the same. To track these problems down, start by moving the target file into the same folder as the current file. Use nothing but the file name in the address. When you link correctly in the same folder, move the target up or down, one level at a time, modifying the `href` value appropriately. Moving up or down just one level at a time can be world's faster than trying to move a few levels (which is an invitation to small errors). Small address errors are fatal, of course. "File not Found" is not a helpful message. Avoid it.

The `<a>` tag also has other attributes such as `id`, (for CSS and JavaScript) and `target`. The `target` lets you decide for your user whether your link should open in the same tab or in a different tab or different window. We don't make that decision for our visitors. They can right-click "Open in New Tab" if they want. Or they can open in the current tab and press the back button when the time comes. You can look up the `target` attribute if you think you know better than your visitors.

Project—Navigating Is Linking

You should turn now to the Companion page, starting with "Three-Page Navigation":

Online: Knowits > HTML I > Online 4

Here you create a quick 3-page "website" and link the pages with an easy-to-use set of navigation links. With that done you can create a fourth page and add it to the "website" or you can go straight to your own project.

Either way, your pages will be nicely linked when you are done and they will start to feel a bit like a website. Congratulations!

Np++ Secrets—Macros, Shortcuts

A "keyboard macro" is a recorded sequence of editing commands. If the editing task is repetitious, record it!

A "keyboard shortcut" is a single letter plus some combination of "modifier" keys that issues a command. In the case of Notepad++, of course, this will be an edit command.

There are lots of keyboard shortcuts, and you probably alread knew many: Ctrl+S to Save, Ctrl+C to Copy to the clipboard, Ctrl+N to create a new file, and so on. You can use Notepad++ to assign any shortcuts you like. Most helpful, you can assign shortcuts to your macros.

This can be very powerful, or it can just be used by picky people, like us, to get things exactly as wanted. Our Save (Ctrl+S), for example, trims trailing blanks and then saves. Do things your way!

Online: Engineers > Frontend Tools > Notepad++ > Macros

Online: Engineers > Frontend Tools > Notepad++ > Shortcuts

Entities—Greek

Greek was favored with the inclusion of its entire alphabet, uppercase and lowercase, as character entities. Now, certainly we love all the descendants of Alexander and Aristotle, but the reason their alphabet was special was because the mathematicians (and mathematical scientists, such as physicists) couldn't seem to talk to each other without it.

Delightfully, the system devised was one you will master in a minute or two. (Master at least to the extent that you know the Greek alphabet.) The Companion page ends with this subject fully explained.

Quiz

Choose the word or phrase that best completes each sentence.

1) The Internet and the World-Wide Web were born
    a) in 1959 and 1969.
    b) together in 1979.
    c) in 1969 and 1989.
    d) in 1969 and 1979.

2) The WWW was created at
    a) U.C. Berkeley.
    b) Stanford (in Silicon Valley).
    c) CERN (in Switzerland).

3) Website navigation should be
    a) fresh and original.
    b) obvious and familiar.
    c) on the right side of that page.

4) Your dictionary should be
    a) an abridged edition, to be handy.
    b) an unabridged edition, to be comprehensive.
    c) online, to be handy and comprehensive.
    d) a search engine, to search multiple dictionaries.

5) To add a title to browsers' tabs you
    a) add a `<title>` to the head section.
    b) start the body section with a `<title>`.
    c) add a `<tab>` title to the head section.
    d) register with the browser companies.

6) The `<br>` tag is
    a) deprecated in HTML 5.
    b) not supported in HTML 5.
    c) supported, but without attributes in HTML 5.

7) The <center> tag is
   a) deprecated in HTML 5.
   b) deprecated in HTML 4 and 5.
   c) not supported in HTML 4, deprecated in HTML 5.
   d) deprecated in HTML 4, not supported in HTML 5.

8) The <a> tag is
   a) always used as an anchor.
   b) always used for linking pages.
   c) optional for linking pages.
   d) used with a link attribute.

9) To link a page with another page in a subfolder you
   a) specify "../" before the subfolder name.
   b) specify the subfolder name, then a "\".
   c) specify the subfolder name, the a "/".
   d) specify a "/", then the subfolder name.

10) The Companion page demonstrates navigation with
   a) ragtime music from the gay '90s.
   b) jazz from the Swing era.
   c) rock and roll from the '50s.
   d) folk music from the '60s.

5 Add a Sense of Time

History—HTML 1, 2, 3

HTML 1 is an unofficial title given to Sir Tim Berners-Lee's first browser (named WorldWideWeb) and documented in a short paper listing its 18 tags and their three attributes. With the invention of the Web, however, the creation of far more impressive browsers followed close on its heels.

Working at the National Center for Supercomputing Applications (NCSA, University of Illinois) Marc Andreesen and collaborators created a browser that was remarkably easy to use, ran on Windows computers (the Web, like the Internet, had been primarily a Unix-based phenomenon) and supported graphics. Some say it made the Web take off.

Leaving academia for the commercial world, Andreesen was one of the founders of Netscape where his next-generation browser, to become Netscape Navigator, took over the browser application market. It sparked a furious commercial contest for browser supremacy that sparked a wide variety of markup languages, all known as HTML and all featuring their own, proprietary enhancements. It became obvious that a single, standard markup language was needed to realize the WWW's initial goals.

The first serious effort to create an industry-wide standard was the Internet Engineering Task Force's effort to standardize HTML 2. A summary paper, RFC 1866, was released in 1995. It failed to reach a consensus and the IETF closed the working group in 1996.

In the meantime, the World-Wide Web Consortium (online at w3.org), with Sir Tim Berners-Lee at its head, was formed and began work on HTML 3. It also failed to reach a consensus.

In the "browser wars" Microsoft fought fiercely against Netscape's market dominance. By bundling its browser with its Windows operating system, Microsoft succeeded in promoting its own Internet Explorer browser to a market-dominating position. While this was going on, the HTML author who wanted most browser users to be able to access a website had to write two (and sometimes more) versions of HTML.

http://www.ncsa.illinois.edu/Projects/mosaic.html NCSA Mosaic

Websites—Changes

The Internet has grown exponentially. Its growth rate may be accelerating. One of the biggest trends today is the trend toward smaller screens.

No, desktop monitors are not getting smaller. They are getting larger and their resolutions (up to 2440 pixels wide) are growing even faster. But the real change is in the other direction. Desktops were long ago joined by laptops. Recently they have been joined by tablets and smart phones. (The earliest "smart" phones were less than 200 pixels wide.) The good news is that HTML lets our pages be viewed on any size screen, so there is no movement to replace HTML with anything else. The bad news is that HTML cannot produce miracles. If your web pages aren't designed for a wide range of sizes, they will not look good outside your design range.

A second trend is toward increasing the variety of input devices. Fingers, for example, are joining mice. The good news there is that scrolling will happen nicely without changing your HTML. Your mouse can drag the elevator car or your fingers can flick it. Browsers handle both.

And the bad news is that you still have to think about the issues. Pages that scroll vertically work well. Pages that scroll horizontally work poorly on the desktop and are worse on a tablet or phone. The time line we start in this chapter will probably need to scroll horizontally.

Should you be worried about these changes? Well, yes. Should you be paralyzed? Of course not. If that time line needs to scroll horizontally, let the viewer scroll! (But be sure that's the exception, not the rule.)

And note that HTML 5 includes support for finger gestures well beyond simply moving a scrollbar. They're ready for you already.

Now, if we go back in time and freeze the web and our browsers when they were all desktops, we would still not freeze our websites. The Companion page has more:

Online: Knowits > HTML I > Online > 5 "Websites—Changes"

Tools—Forums

There are online forums for HTML (and for almost every other topic under the sun). If you've not visited forums yet, you are missing out.

You have a problem. You post a question. You get answers! It's nearly magic. Here are some hints.

Appropriate answers: you are just beginning? Identify yourself as a newbie. "Hi. I'm new at this so..." Most forum participants will be kinder and provide more detailed answers to newbies.

You tried code and it doesn't work? Post a few lines of your HTML along with the problem. Most fixes are obvious. Most forum participants are delighted to help when they see that you are trying.

Try searching for answers first! Your best friend is your search engine. Ask it a question. Your forums have search boxes. Use them. "I'm a newbie and I've searched for..." will get you very specific help. And the other forum folk will appreciated your good manners.

Do you want abuse? Nothing annoys forum volunteers like the posters whose homework is late, who haven't tried anything on their own and who haven't searched for an answer because they haven't got to a problem (except that their homework is late).

So do choose a forum and ask a question. Do you get a prompt and friendly answer? That's your forum! Does tomorrow arrive with your question not answered? Try another forum.

You can contact us, too. We enjoy hearing from you. We do not, however, provide individual technical help. (Sorry.) One exception: did we overlook something? If it's not in the syllabus—see the menu!--perhaps we should add it. Tell us.

Head—`<link>`

When you look at other sites HTML (you right-click the page and View Source) you will see `<link>` tags (no closing tag) in the head section. What do they mean?

If there are CSS styles for the page you are viewing, they will be between `<style>` and `</style>` tags in the head section. If the site is larger, they will be in a separate CSS file and it will be referenced with a `<link>` tag in the head section. This is the one we use in the chapter Companion pages:

```
    <link rel='stylesheet'
type='text/css'
href='../../../../../support/css/mr.css
'>
```

Of course, you won't need to link CSS pages until you learn some CSS, which is the topic of Volume II. But you may want to link your favicon (which we cover in this volume—it's coming soon). So here are the parts:

- rel—the relationship of the linked page
- type—the type of content of the linked page
- href—the address of the linked page

To link your favicon (that's the little 16 by 16 pixel icon in the browser tabs) you use rel='shortcut icon'. Here's ours:

```
<link rel='shortcut icon'
href='http://www.MartinRinehart.com/fav
icon.ico'
>
```

(No need for a type if the rel is shortcut icon.) We'll give you an example again when we get there.

Blocks—Tables, Outlines

Ready for that time line? It's just a fancy table. This chapter starts with the table basics. We'll add more in the next chapter and we'll get fancy in Chapter 9. Later in this chapter we'll show you how to add a basic table for your site's time line.

First, a bit of reading. Let's begin at the beginning.

The <table> Tag

You start a table with the <table> tag; you end it with the </table> closing tag. Some attributes you should know are:

- bgcolor
- border
- cellpadding

(This is a partial list. If it's not all you want, google for more.)

We covered the bgcolor attribute in Chapter 3. Your <body> may have a light color background, or you may leave it white (or whatever color your visitor specified). We recommend that you always add a bit of color, but a very light one, to your table's background. It helps the table stand out. We're partial to #f0f0ff, a nice, light blue.

The border specifies the width of the surrounding border and the width of the bars between rows and columns, in pixels. One is usually enough.

The cellpadding is the space, also in pixels, between the border bars and the content of the cells. If you leave it out, the text or numbers in the cells will touch the borders, which does not look good. Three pixels is a nice padding. You can leave more if you've got plenty of space.

There is also a cellspacing attribute. We seldom use it but you'll want to try it on your own, to see how it differs from cellpadding.

If you don't specify the width attribute the table will be wide enough for its content, which is usually what you want. Forcing a wider width is certainly possible, but are you sure your viewer's monitor is as wide as yours? You could have viewers with tablets or cell phones. Browsers scrunch tables, normally intelligently, if they are too wide. You might want to insert `<br>` tags into your wider cells, to get breaks where you want them.

The `<tr>` Tag

You can look at a table as a set of rows divided into columns. Or you can look at it as a set of columns divided into rows. HTML chose the former. A table is a set of rows, as a list is a set of list items. You nest `<tr>` ... `</tr>` tags within `<table>` ... `</table>` tags.

The `<tr>` tag has several attributes, the only one of which we use regularly is the `bgcolor` attribute. See Chapter 3 if you want a refresher.

In an earlier era of data processing, reports were printed on "green-bar" paper. That was paper with alternating green (a light green that didn't conflict with the letters printed on it) and white bars running across the page, each tall enough for three report lines. This made it easy to trace a report line from the far right back to the far left.

It is still a good way to make wide reports more readable, especially if there is horizontal scrolling required. (Don't forget: some of your viewers will have narrower devices than the monitor you work at.) Three lines of `'#f0fff0'` alternating with three lines of white works on a report with a `'#f0f0ff'` background.

The `<td>` Tag

Finally, we get our table's content in "table datum" cells. The `<td>` … `</td>` cells nest within the `<tr>` … `</tr>` tags.

You'll probably use the `<td>`'s `bgcolor` attribute. You'll also need to specify the `align` attribute (`'left'`, `'center'` or `'right'`--the default `'left'` works for data like names, but you need `'right'` for a column of numbers). The `valign` attribute (vertical align—`'top'`, `'middle'` or `'bottom'`) can come in handy. Also, we often specify `width` (e.g., `width='100px'`).

The examples in this chapter's Project section will give you some practice in making tables. We'll do more in Chapter 6 and Chapter 9. (Time lines are very demanding. That's why we chose one for our sample project.)

Outlines

You already know how to do an outline (if you've thought about it). You start with an ordered list, capital Roman numerals (`<ol type='I'>`). Inside the list items, you add more lists (`<ol type='A'>`). Inside those, you add more lists (`<ol type='1'>`). And you could go on to lowercase Roman and English letters, too.

But this can get confusing. The Companion page shows you a trick to keep the whole thing simple.

Online: Knowits > HTML I > Online > 5 "Outlines"

Inline—Corrections

The three inline tags here can be used to mark changes in an HTML document, in the same way a word processing document can be marked up in a group effort. Alternatively, you can make a permanent record of revisions a part of your page. "The former rule read `<del>` old rule here `</del>` but this was changed to `<ins>` new rule here `</ins>`."

The `<del>` Tag

Marks deleted text.

The `<ins>` Tag

Marks inserted text. Often follows deleted text. Commonly marked by underscoring the inserted text.

The `<s>` Tag

Marks text to be shown with strike through. Formerly this was `<strike>`. In current browsers `<del>` and `<s>` text may be the same.

An example of these is shown at:

Online: Knowits > HTML I > Online > 5 "Inline" topic

Project—A Time Line Table

At this point, take a good look at the time line in our sample project.

Online: Knowits > HTML I > Project > "Timeline" page

Note first that the horizontal bars are continuous; there are no table borders here. Look at the time line row. It has small cells in the 16th and 18th centuries, larger cells in the 17th. Yes, those are headings and text paragraphs below the time line row but they are very much in the table.

The simple table tags we've introduced will get your time line page started. We've got two more chapters with heavy doses of tables to get to a really nice result.

For now, back to the Companion page and start on your own. You'll make a sample time line before you start on your project's time line.

Online: Knowits > HTML I > Online > 5

A quick note on our history. Berners-Lee invented the WWW in 1989. HTML 4 became official in 1997; HTML 4.01 in 1999. HTML 5 is with us today, but not yet an official W3C "Recommendation." The HTML Living Standard from WHATWG incorporates all of the W3Cs HTML 5, and is a current standard (so, in a broader sense, HTML 5 is already a standard).

But hold on. Those are history facts from our next five chapters. We'll get there. For now, our sample time line is roughly accurate. That's what you want for your project's time line: a nice visual representation that gives your viewers an overall impression. (Galileo is early; Newton is late).

Np++ Secrets—Tabs

Have you noticed how we indent our listings:

```
<ul>
    <li>This is</li>
    <li>an indented</li>
    <li>unordered list.</li>
</ul>
```

Indenting is vital to writing readable computer code, in every language we have ever used (and that's quite a few). It is seldom meaningful to the computer. Browsers don't care how (or if) you indent your HTML. But it certainly makes your life easier when you have to edit it.

Notepad++ can help you make friends with the tab key, which makes indenting a pleasure.

Online: Engineers > Frontend Tools > Notepad++ > More
Np++ > Tabs

Entities—Currency Symbols

After the perfectly wonderful way the Greek alphabet is made available through character entities, you can't help but be disappointed in the paltry selection of currency symbols. In addition to the dollar sign, you have four other choices. On the bright side, you'll learn them almost instantly.

Online: Knowits > HTML I > Online > 5

If you are one of the five billion or so people offended by the lack of consideration for your own currency, well, we don't blame you. You might express your feelings to the W3C. Perhaps you could send a "thank you" note to Sir Tim for all his contributions, and then add a P. S.

Quiz

Choose the word or phrase that best completes each sentence.

1) HTML 1, 2 and 3 have this in common
    a) They specified earlier versions of HTML.
    b) They specified HTML dialects prior to 1990.
    c) They didn't exist.

2) The size ratio between the widest and narrowest devices is
    a) over 10 to1.
    b) about 8 to 1.
    c) over 5 to 1.
    d) under 3 to 1.

3) Online HTML forums are least helpful if you
    a) research before you post a question.
    b) include a bit of HTML in your post.
    c) state that you are a newbie.
    d) are overdue with an assignment.

4) The `<link>` tag
    a) must be matched with an `</link>` tag.
    b) can include `rel`, `type` and `href` attributes.
    c) can include `rel`, `src` and `alt` attributes.
    d) goes at the bottom of the body section.

5) The `bgcolor` attribute can be used with
    a) `<table>` and `<tr>` tags.
    b) `<tr>` and `<td>` tags.
    c) `<table>` and `<td>` tags.
    d) `<table>`, `<tr>` and `<td>` tags.

6) The `<table>` tag may include these attributes
    a) `bgcolor`, `width` and `src`.
    b) `border`, `width` and `src`.
    c) `border`, `cellpadding` and `width`.
    d) `bgcolor`, `border`, `cellpadding`, `width` and more.

7) The content of an individual row/column table intersection is
    a) a `<tcell>` value.
    b) a `<tc>` value.
    c) a `<td>` value.
    d) a `<te>` value.

8) The `valign` attribute values are
    a) the same as the `align` attribute values.
    b) specified in pixels.
    c) specified in pixels or percents.
    d) `'top'`, `'middle'` or `'bottom'`.

9) The `<del>` and `<s>` tags show
    a) diagonal and vertical strikeout marks, respectively.
    b) horizontal and vertical strikeout marks, respectively.
    c) are different in different browsers.
    d) defined differently in HTML 5.

10) One currency with a convenient character entity is the
    a) franc.
    b) mark.
    c) yen.
    d) yuan.

6 Populate Your Site

In this chapter we're going to create an image map for your project site. This is generally regarded as an advanced feature, which is unfortunate. Image maps are very useful, and well worth doing. If you do not recall the map on our sample site, take another look:

Online: Knowits > HTML I > Project > Map

Compare the map to a text statement that says, "these scientists were spread out, geographically." Pictures can explain things clearly!

An image map doesn't have to be an image of a map. For example, you could start with a group portrait (think Rembrandt's *Nightwatch*) and combine it with a map that would tell you a little about each person as your mouse pointer hovered.

Now, time to open the Companion page and get started.

Online: Knowits > HTML I > Online > 6

This chapter's history lesson begins the saga of HTML's standardization, a topic important to everyone who uses this markup language.

History—HTML Standardized

It was the middle of the 1990s, Netscape Navigator and Microsoft Internet Explorer were fighting for market dominance and the poor HTML author was caught in the middle, essentially writing two separate dialects of one markup language.

At the World-Wide Web Consortium (W3C), longtime HTML proponent Dave Raggett took over writing and shepherding through what became HTML 3.2, the first official HTML standard. While it provided a single *de jure* standard for HTML, the HTML author had to write and test HTML for both Navigator and Internet Explorer browsers. To make matters worse, MSIE 4 (1996) was only partially compatible with MSIE 5 (1999). Writing HTML that would run in all the popular browsers ("cross-browser" programming) was a challenge.

While the situation is much better today than it was a decade ago, cross-browser programming is still one of the frontend engineer's main challenges.

http://www.nethistory.info/History%20of%20the %20Internet/browserwars.html Browser wars

Websites—Visitors

Some websites have a strictly defined audience. If you coach youth soccer you may have a site for your team with practice times, game schedule and so on. Your audience is your team members. Get the facts right on your site and you will spend a lot less time on the phone.

Other sites, however, have to work much harder to find an audience. An information site, such as our project site and your project site, too, has to give visitors a reason to take a look. Once they take a look, it has to answer their needs or they will move on.

If they click on an information site, it's because they want information. They probably googled their topic. They found your site because it was information-rich and SEO-savvy. Good work! Once they find your site, why will they stay?

Your home page is what marketers call a "landing page." Your prospective visitor sees your ad. It's interesting. Click! Now what?

Your home page is your landing page. If it's a good one, it gets another click. Our sample has portraits, a time line and a map. Maybe the visitor wants to know more about Descartes or who was youngest or where these folks lived. It's there on the landing page (home page, too).

Would you have guessed that these scientists were spread all over Europe in an age when they could only communicate by snail mail? And if you think snail mail is slow today, imagine what it was like back then. We were really quite surprised when we made this map. That probably gets some visitor's clicks, too.

Your map should do the same. And if it does, then you ask yourself if every other page can be just as interesting. Go to work on the dullest one first. If you keep working on the dullest page, pretty soon you won't have any dull pages. Hello, visitors!

Tools—Image Maps

An image map is simply an image with a map (not visible) superimposed on top of it. The map is simply a set of shapes with coordinates that locate the shapes. In our map we located "Newton" (the text label, not the scientist) outside London, roughly over Cambridge, where he did much of his work.

We specified that "Newton" was a rectangle. It was 172 pixels in from the left side of the image, and so on. How did we know that it was 172 pixels from the left? An image map tool helped us with the coordinates.

These tools all let you supply an image, move a mouse pointer over the image and the tools report, in some more or less helpful fashion, the coordinates. A helpful report will let you copy/paste the coordinates from the map tool into your HTML.

Many of these tools are commercial products. Many let you try them for free. If you are going to make many image maps, they can be worthwhile investments. (Good workmen are not afraid to invest in good tools.) But for your first map, keep your money.

The Companion page lists some map tools. You can google for more.

Head—`<base>`, `<script>`

Here we'll cover that `<base>` tag, which makes it easy to move your site from the local machine you use for development to an ISP that will host your site for the world at large. We'll cover `<script>` (which shouldn't really be in the head-section, but often is). Last, we'll cover `<noscript>` which is closely related to `<script>`, though it's never in the head-section.

The `<base>` Tag

When you build a website on a Windows computer, you might start in a folder such as c:\website_project. When you get a site from an ISP, it will be identified by URL: www.WebsiteProject.com and will be located (likely, but check with your ISP) at the root folder: /. (Note that even the slash is different: backward in Windows, forward at your Linux-based ISP.) The `<base>` tag lets you assign a relative base address (such as c:\webasite_project) while you create your site, and then change to the ISP's root, /, when you upload to your ISP. All you have to change is the content of your `<base>`.

(We use a bit of script that detects whether we're working in the office or running on the ISP, so we don't have to change anything at all, which is even more convenient but you will need to get at least through Volume III of this series to do that.)

The `<script>` Tag

When you get there, you will put your first JavaScript between `<script>` and `</script>` tags. We hope you will put the script at the end of the body section, which is now considered best. It used to be the best practice to put the script in the head section, where you will still find it in older sites, or in sites with less well-informed HTML authors. When you get there (Volume III of this series) you'll find that you can also use the `<script>` tag to link to JavaScript in a stand-alone file.

To be correct, any script in any language can go between `<script>` and `</script>` tags. To be practical, JavaScript is the only language understood by all modern browsers, so JavaScript is the only sensible language choice.

The `<noscript>` Tag

Suppose your visitor does not have JavaScript enabled? (It's available in all modern browsers, but the hyper-nervous type might turn it off for better security. More likely, the hyper-nervous corporate IT department might turn it off to keep the employee's noses to the grindstone.) Without JavaScript the browsers will ignore the content between `<script>` and `</script>`. Instead, they will display the content between `<noscript>` and `</noscript>` tags. This content will almost always be placed in the body-section and will almost always say something like, "You can't properly view this site without JavaScript." (That will be said more politely than the JavaScript author feels it should be said, we hope.) Some sites will have alternate content just for the one percent or so who do not have JavaScript enabled.

Blocks—`<addr>`, Rows

The `<addr>` Tag

Formerly important (when the WWW hyperlinked academic papers) the `<addr>` and `</addr>` tags enclosed the author's snail mail address. Browsers may, but seldom do, provide special formatting for this block. If you use it you will be able to provide your own special formatting when you learn some CSS.

Table Captions—`<caption>`

You can place a caption on top of the table (call it row zero) if you follow specific rules. You use a `<caption>` and `</caption>` pair to surround your caption. This pair must be the first thing following the `<table>` tag. Your browser will format the caption but a little help would probably be a good idea. You might use `<strong>` emphasis, for instance.

Table Row Groups—`<thead>`, `<tbody>`, `<tfoot>`

The `<thead>`, `<tbody>` and `<tfoot>` blocks group (or would group, if they were implemented) the rows of a table into head, body and footer sections. This at least seems like a useful idea. For example, if the table were long you might want the `<thead>` section to repeat on every page.

Well, you might want to use these groups, but your browsers don't use them. Dividing your tables with these seemingly helpful group tags has no effect today, save for one exception we note below. It might help in the future, and it certainly should be important to non-visual browsers, so go ahead and use these tags, if you like. They won't hurt.

The exception will not hit you until you start writing JavaScript. Then you will find that attaching table rows to a table won't work. You have to attach the rows to a table body, which is, in turn, attached to the table. This will not be on your quizzes in this volume. Remembering it will, however, help you escape from a mean, mystery bug if you go on to write JavaScript. (Can you guess how we learned this?)

Column Headers—`<th>`

Not, in fact, a table row, the `<th>` cells (table headers, not `<thead>`, though) is a cell that you place on top of a column. As a header, almost always part of a row of `<th>` cells, this does what you might do anyway: it presents your header in emphasized text, often boldface, and centers it over the column. Just as important (or perhaps more important) it gives an aural browser something helpful to say, such as "in the column headed 'xxx'...". Start most of your columns with `<th>` cells, not `<td>` cells. This is illustrated in the Companion page:

Online: Knowits > HTML I > Online > 6

Inline—Emphasis

Here we'll cover two tags that are very simple but often not used correctly. Done professionally, these tags will replace presentational elements with correct semantic elements.

The `<em>` Tag

How do you emphasize important words? By putting them in italics? With boldface?

The correct answer is neither; you let the browser take care of presentation after you take care of semantics. The `<em>` and `</em>` tags surround text that you want to emphasize. You let the browser (which may be visual, aural or it be be showing your words in braille) emphasize the text.

The `<strong>` Tag

Suppose you want some text even more strongly emphasized? The `<strong>` tag is your tool. The name is an abbreviation for "even more strongly emphasized than `<em>` text."

There are legitimate reasons for using presentational tags, such as `<i>` (for italic). For example, in a bibliography the names of books should be shown in italics. This is a presentational requirement, correctly handled with a presentational tag.

Being professionals, we know the difference. These are also illustrated in your Companion page.

Project—Make Your Map

Our sample project uses a map of Europe as the image under an image map. It's important that you distinguish the two.

An image map, in HTML, is an invisible map which you use on top of an actual image graphic. The graphic may be a map, or it may be a group portrait from your last family reunion. Assume it is the latter. You use tracing paper over the photo. Trace neatly around the head of Aunt Polly, Trace neatly around the head of Uncle Tom, and around Scottie, your sheep dog. These tracings are the image map. You will convert them to HTML, discard the tracing paper and overlay the photo with the HTML map.

Here we'll explain exactly how this is done, and then we'll send you to the Companion page where you'll be directed to build your own for your project website.

The Image `<map>`

An image map is content between `<map>` and `</map>` tags, plus the `<map name=...>` attribute. The `<map>` is a container for `<area>`s. Each `<area>` is an `<area>` tag (no `</area>`) with the details of one area on the underlying image. There are two simple ways to define map areas, and one complex one (that we do not recommend). Your choices are:

- `circle` a circular area

- `rect` a rectangular area

- `poly` a precisely defined polygonal area

This is the code for the Isaac Newton area of our sample project:

```
<area
    alt="link to Newton page"
    coords="172,172,249,203"
    href="newton.html"
    shape="rect"
    title="Sir Isaac Newton, taught in
Cambridge"
>
```

The attributes of an area combine attributes of an image (`alt`, for alternative text for a non-visual browsers, `title` for a tooltip) with the `href` attribute of a `<link>` or `<a>` tag. Additionally, you specify the shape (`circle`, `rect` or `poly`) and the `coords` that define the shape.

For a circular area, the `coords` are the x and y coordinates of the center of the circle plus the radius, in pixels, of the circle. For a rectangle the coordinates are the x and y of the top-left corner, and the x and y of the bottom-right corner, in pixels. A polygon requires an x and y coordinate for each point along its perimeter.

Specifying polygons is tedious work, and of dubious value for this application. Image maps are typically used so the visitor can click on something and be directed to a relevant page. Precise polygons are more useful for, for example, a photo editing package where you want to precisely outline an area to extract or mask out. (Do you really want your visitor directed to page A with one click or page B with a click just one pixel away?)

Overlaying Your Image

Connecting an image with a map could hardly be simpler. This is the relevant HTML from our project:

```
<img... usemap='#europe'...>

<map name='europe'> ... </map>
```

Note that the name for the `usemap` attribute is prefixed with a # symbol. You'll see this again when you link to a named anchor within a page.

Now it's your turn:

Online: Knowits > HTML I > Online > 6 "Sample Project"

You should get a very nice page to add to your project.

Np++ Secrets—Find in Files

Suppose you decide to change something in your site, something that requires changing not just one HTML file, but it requires changing one file for each page. Tedious work?

Maybe not! The "Find in Files" feature doesn't just find, it also replaces. ("Find and/or Replace in Files" is more accurate, but it doesn't fit on most browser tabs.) If you can describe your change with a Find/Replace dialog, you can fix your entire site at once:

Online: Engineers > Frontend Tools >

Notepad++ > More Np++ > Find in Files

Entities—Ligatures

In English, two adjacent letters were sometimes combined to form a new "letter" called a "ligature." The age of the typewriter, with which true ligatures were not possible, nearly killed this delightful echo of times past.

If you believe that Newton's *Philosophiæ Naturalis Principia Mathematica* deserves to be spelled out with some reverence (including *Philosophiæ)* you will enjoy this one:

Online: Knowits > HTML I > Online > 6 > "Ligatures" section

(This is for pleasure only. Ligatures will not be on our quizzes.)

Quiz

Choose the word or phrase that best completes each sentence.

1) In the mid-1990s, the two major browsers were
    a) Netscape Navigator and NCSA Mosaic.
    b) Microsoft Internet Explorer and NCSA Mosaic.
    c) MSIE 4 and MSIE 5.
    d) MSIE and Netscape Navigator.

2) HTML's first official standard was written by
    a) Dave Raggett.
    b) Marc Andreesen.
    c) Tim Berners-Lee.

3) An image map is
    a) a map with images (such as pictures of people) on top.
    b) a picture (such as of a person) with a map on top.
    c) an invisible map on top of an image.
    d) an invisible image with a visible map on top.

4) A `<base>` tag provides
    a) a relative address from which other addresses are specified.
    b) an absolute address from which other addresses are specified.
    c) the address of your home page.
    d) a synonym for a site's URL.

5) The `<script>` tag
    a) is used in the head section.
    b) is used in the body section.
    c) should start the body section.
    d) may appear anywhere, but it should end the body section.

6) The `<noscript>` tag
a) is used in the head section if there is no `<script>` tag.
b) is used in the body section if there is no `<script>` tag.
c) is used in the body section if there is a `<script>` tag.
d) may be used in the body section for browsers that have scripting disabled.

7) An image will use a map
a) if a `<map>` tag is present.
b) if `<area>`s have been defined before the `</img>` tag.
c) if `<area>`s have been defined after the `</img>` tag.
d) if a usemap attribute specifies # followed by a map name.

8) A map contains
a) names and attributes of shapes.
b) a name and nested `<area>` tags.
c) nested `<area>` ... `</area>` content.
d) a name and nested `<area>` ... `</area>` content.

9) A map may contain
a) circles, squares or polygons.
b) ovals, rectangles or polygons.
c) ovals, squares or rectangles.
d) circles, rectangles or polygons.

10) A `<strong>` tag describes
a) a good morning coffee.
b) text that should have moderate emphasis.
c) text that should be stronger than emphasized text.
d) text that is only weaker than `<stronger>` text.

7 It Takes a Village

In this chapter we'll add anchors and intra-page links to our website projects. Before then, our History will march forward to HTML 4.01, which is still the reigning HTML standard despite being thirteen years old. After that we'll take a look at the "village" of engineers that are required to build a website, and we'll look at new blocks and six inline presentation elements. To start, open to the Companion page:

Online: Knowits > HTML I > Online > 7

History—HTML 4[.01] Lasts

In late 1997 the W3C published the "Recommendation" (W3C jargon for "official standard") for HTML 4. This was superseded in December, 1999, by the HTML 4.01 Recommendation. (As the version numbers suggest, 4.01 made only minor fixes and improvements over version 4.) The 4.01 version was, and still is, the official HTML standard. (HTML 5 is now at "last call" stage, the final step before becoming a Recommendation.)

The XHTML standards (1 and 1.1) included, by reference, the HTML 4.01 standard for tags and attributes.

For the 21st century we have spoken of "standards-based" HTML which means HTML 4.01. As a practical matter, today we have HTML 4.01 and three versions of MSIE (8, 9 and 10) for a total of four versions of HTML. While the version differences are frustrating to frontend engineers, they are minor compared to the old differences from the days of the "browser wars."

On the website, see the Engineer's track, HTML topic for extensive tables comparing HTML versions from 1 through 5.

See the Companion page for a clickable link to the official 4.01 standard.

Websites—Frontenders

In 2008, Hillary Rodham Clinton (wife of President W. J. Clinton—then, herself, candidate for President) published a book titled *It Takes a Village* from an old African saying, "It takes a village to raise a child." (This was controversial. American conservatives saw it as an argument for intrusive government programs. Republican presidential nominee Bob Dole said, "...it does not take a village to raise a child.") Here, we refer to the "village" of engineers it takes to create a website (and leave the arguments over rearing children to others).

Alan Cooper, designer/architect of Microsoft's Visual Basic wrote a book provocatively titled *The Inmates Are Running the Asylum*. This is the original source for much of the thinking in this field. (It is one of those rare books that has not lost any relevance in the years since it was new.)

Information Architecture

The overall flow of information is designed by the information architect(s). What data is needed from the visitor? All at once, from a single form, or some on one page and more on another page, as required?

Of course, websites that collect information require backend engineers to connect the information entered to the backend database. We decided on an educational-only site from the outset, as we are covering HTML, a frontend concern, and leaving the backend engineering for another day (or, perhaps, for other engineers). With an educational site, the information architecture is relatively simple: how do we divide our subject into pages?

User Interface / User Experience

With an information architecture in place, we turn to the UI/UX specialist(s). How do we make our site fun for the visitors? Even with an educational site, such as our project sites, tools such as image maps help. The visitors click and are whisked away to a relevant page to satisfy their curiosity.

Design

Once the UI/UX design is done, we turn to the designer(s). Used by itself, the word "design" when applied to websites (and web applications) refers specifically to the artistic elements: what colors? What layout? This is a very complex art form, as it must function well, in addition to looking good. (Imagine da Vinci when you say, "Lisa looks good, Leo. Now, we want the visitor to click on various parts to learn more about her.")

And now, for those of you who prefer rugged individualism (or simply have no other choice) we settle the "it takes a village" argument, conclusively. If you haven't got a village, you do it yourself. You wear lots of different hats.

In the next two chapters we'll explore some others who might be helpful in your "village." There is more on this village at:

Online: Engineers > Frontend Team

Tools—Validators

The W3C maintains "validators" to help us with our code. You simply supply the address of a page and it will be checked for errors. When your page is error free, you can affix the official W3C emblem.

The W3C validators have been gathered under one head, "Unicorn Validator" (where "unicorn" should remind you of "unified"). This will check your HTML and CSS, and even your RSS feeds, all in just one place.

These validators are helpful and they are not nearly as popular as they should be. We highly recommend that you take advantage of this service. It will definitely help you catch errors in your work.

That said, we are not W3C validator fans. They are better than nothing, but not nearly as helpful as they should be.

First, there are errors in the validators. For example, if your page starts with a comment (a good practice) the validators will not accept it as valid HTML. (Starting with a comment is perfectly valid.)

Second, and more importantly, the HTML is validated as correct SGML, the markup language standard on which HTML was based. Valid SGML may be ridiculous HTML. Try these:

```
<table … width='not too wide, please'>
```

```
<table … width='100lightyears'>
```

These are both valid SGML (which requires that an attribute value be quoted, if it's text, but doesn't care what the text content contains).

You will find a clickable link on the Companion page. You can bookmark the Unicorn Validator, or just remember "Unicorn Validator."

Head—Vital Meta

For this chapter, and the rest of the knowit, we're going to add the `<meta>` tags to our coverage of tags in the head section. The first bit of good news here is that we've already covered all the other head section tags. The second bit of good news is that the critical `<meta>` tags will all go in our templates, so you'll have nothing to remember, nothing to add. Start your pages with a good template and you're in business.

name="author"

The first of our four "name" meta tags is the one you use to claim credit for your work:

```
<meta name="author" content="Betsy
Ross">
```

Of course, you'll want to make a small change to the above if your name is not "Betsy Ross." This tag is not vital, but it's nice to see, especially if the name is your own.

name="description"

This tag is vital. When the Google search engine recommends sites that meet a searcher's criteria, the description on the SERP (search-engine results page) is taken from this tag, if there is one. (Otherwise, the search engine does its best to write a description. It does quite a good job, if you allow for the fact that it's a computer program.) So:

```
<meta name="description" content="The
way I want my site described on the
SERP. Proper punctuation and
capitalization included.">
```

For practical restrictions on the length of the description, do a search and check the site descriptions.

name="generator"

If a program generates your HTML it will likely use its name as the value of the `content` attribute in this tag. The vital fact is that you not have one. (Fill a page in your word processor with Lorem Ipsum and then Save As... HTML to see an example.)

name="keywords"

In the olden days (last century) search engines looked at the keywords listed in this tag. Did they match the words in a search? The site was a valid result.

Still in those olden days, unscrupulous webmasters entered dishonest lists of keywords, getting their sites included where they did not belong. Search engines figured this scam out. They dropped these keywords from their results criteria. Some even lowered the rankings of sites simply because they included keywords.

Today, we always include keywords. (Separate "words" with commas. The "words" may be multi-word phrases.) Be sure that your keywords in this tag are also words in places such as the site title, in H1 headings and image `alt` descriptions. At worst, your site will not be penalized. At best, search engines may resume using these words as one minor factor, and you'll be a little better off for taking the small amount of trouble.

htttp-equiv=

In Chapters 8 and 9 the whole "Head" section is devoted to additional meta tags, about half of the `http-equiv=`. Some of them don't work (which is important to know); some are useful (which may be important). This chapter's choice is mandatory.

```
<meta http-equiv="content-type"
content="text/html; charset='UTF-8'">
```

This will be repeated in your Companion page where you will embed it into your template. What's it all about?

The `http-equiv` attribute is the HyperText Transfer Protocol equivalent. Normally, a server sends an appropriate HTTP heading along with each page it serves. (These headings precede the HTML pages you create.) Sometimes there is no server, so there is no HTTP header. Most commonly, there is no server when you are creating pages, viewing them as they appear on your hard disk. Other times, such as when you upload your pages to an Internet Service Provider, you have no control over the HTTP headers. If you have an `http-equiv` meta tag, this takes precedence over the actual HTTP header, so you are back in control.

Content of an HTML page is `text/html`, which is the default. It's probably not helpful, but it's tidy and thorough.

The character set should always be `UTF-8`. The Companion page links to explanations of this fact, if you refuse to take advice without knowing the underlying reasons. Warning: the underlying reasons are not simple and the linked pages are not a quick read. You may want to take this one on faith. The default character set may be the common `Latin-1` which you want to replace with `UTF-8`. Be sure you always include this one. Again, we'll bake it into the template and you can forget about it, confident that it is always there.

Blocks—Quotes, `<dl>`

Here we cover the `<blockquote>` tag that you use for block quotes—the long passages you quote from your favorite authors. Then we stay in academia to provide the little used, but still useful, definition list.

Block Quotes

Block quotes are those quotes that are too long to put into the text, surrounded by quotation marks. They are typically indented, both left and right. You include these between `<blockquote>` and `</blockquote>` tags. Leave the exact formatting to the browsers.

You may enclose the citation in a citation attribute, but it will not appear on your page. Better to have a separate citation in your text: "As President [name] said in his [speech name/location] on [date]:". (If you are writing an academic paper, consult your school's recommended style guide for proper footnote form.)

Definition Lists

A definition list is used to define terms. It is similar to the ordered and unordered lists, except that the content provides for both the term being defined and the definition of the term, this way:

```
<dl>
    <dt>cat</dt> <dd>a feline mammal,
frequently residing with humans</dd>
    <dt>dog</dt> <dd>a canine mammal,
frequently domesticated</dd>
</dl>
```

The Companion page has examples of both block quotes and definition lists.

Inline Presentation Tags

The following six tags are all presentational. Avoid them if there is a valid semantic alternative.

<b>, <i> and <u>

These three tags specify bold, italic and underscored text. Use them if they are required for a specific presentation. For example, names of art works should be written in italics in English (such as novels, paintings or movies— Charles Dickens wrote *A Tale of Two Cities*). Do not use these tags when there is a valid semantic alternative, such as <em> or <strong> for adding emphasis.

<big> and <small>

Specifying font sizes, for example, using CSS is a far better alternative. Use these tags to wrap text before you learn a little CSS. You'll abandon them quickly if you learn some CSS.

`<s>` (`<strike>`)

The `<s>` and `<strike>` tags both specify text with a strike-through style. In many browsers these are the same as `<del>` text. As early as HTML 3.2, a note states that `<strike>` may be replaced by `<s>`. Both were deprecated (in favor of CSS) in HTML 4. `<s>` was redefined, in HTML 5, as the correct markup for text that was struck through but not intended for deletion while text marked `<del>` was going to be deleted.

A good first source for fine distinctions like these:

Online: Engineers > HTML >

Database Data > Research Tables > Tag History

`<sub>` and `<sup>`

To create unlimited subscripts and superscripts (not just the three named character entity superscripts) you have the `<sub>` and `<sup>` tags (closed with corresponding end tags. The named character entities are easier, but superscripts can go as high as you like. Examples:

- `&sup3;` same as `<sup>3</sup>`
- no alternative for `<sup>4</sup>`

Project—Your Template

We have two "Project" sections this time, the first very simple (and very important). We add the `<meta>` tags discussed above to create a reasonably complete template. (We will discuss more `<meta>` tags in the next two chapters. You may wish to add some to your template. Your choice.) Our suggestion includes the acronym "SERP," which is the SEO specialists shorthand for Search Engine Results Page. Never forget SEO.

Online: Knowits > HTML I > Online > 7 "Completing the Template"

Project—Linking In-Page

Over time the fine art of linking to a specific spot within a page seems to be getting lost. Why?

We suspect that the reason is that you can only trust the intra-page anchors that you provide for yourself. Linking to a spot in another site's page depends on the other site maintaining the anchor to which you link. Foreign page anchors are notoriously untrustworthy.

In fact, even your own anchors are untrustworthy. Six months from now, will you remember that you've linked to those spots from other pages? Well, you might.

HTML 5 makes it possible to link to spots even though you haven't provided explicit anchors. Don't do it! If you see explicit anchors they will probably make you scratch your head and ask yourself, "Self, why did I put in those anchors?" (Plus, you get to use the <a> tag as an actual anchor, which makes its name a lot more sensible than when you use it for a link.)

The Companion page shows how this is done. Try some links within your own site. (Don't worry if you have no Isaac Newton writing Latin that you fake with lorem ipsum. You can have Jane Austen or your sheepdog speaking lorem ipsum, if you like.)

Np++ Secrets—Bookmarks

We're not big fans of browser bookmarks. It seems like you never have enough, or, when you get more aggressive about bookmarking, you have far too many. Notepad++, on the other hand, has a very different kind of bookmark and we use them constantly.

Warning: once you have used Notepad++ bookmarks you will never be happy with any text editor that lacks this feature.

Entities—Fractions

If you are doing carpentry in the U.S. (where the smallest unit of measure is the inch—just over 2.5cm) you need to use halves and quarters commonly. You can specify these with character entity fractions. (American carpenters also need to measure to the nearest eighth or sixteenth of an inch, for which there are no character entities. Outside the U.S., carpenters measure in millimeters, which don't need fractions.)

The companion page shows the most common (and only, sorry to say) character entity fractions.

Quiz

Choose the word or phrase that best completes each sentence.

1) The current official standard, HTML 4.01, became a W3C Recommendation in
    a) 1989.
    b) 1999.
    c) 2009.

2) HTML 4.01 is the official standard for tags and attributes in
    a) HTML.
    b) XHTML.
    c) both HTML and XHTML.

3) The abbreviations UI / UX stand for
    a) uniform introversion, uniform extroversion.
    b) user interface, user experience.
    c) unified interface, unified experience.

4) To find the W3C validators online, google for "w3c" and
    a) unicorn.
    b) validator.
    c) uniform.
    d) uniform validators.

5) In the tag `<meta name='description' content='xxx'>`, the xxx
    a) specifies the page's character set.
    b) specifies the page's language.
    c) specifies text that can be used for search results pages.
    d) describes the page's presentation.

6) In the tag `<meta http-equiv=...>` the `http-equiv` is

    a) used by the server to send a page header.
    b) used by browsers when there is no page header.
    c) used by browsers to supersede the page header.
    d) both b) and c), above.

7) In HTML 5 you specify text that is going to be deleted with

    a) the `<s>` tag.
    b) the `<strike>` tag.
    c) the `<del>` tag.
    d) any of the above.

8) Links within an `<a>` tag are specified

    a) by name within the `href` attribute.
    b) by name within the `target` attribute.
    c) by a # followed by name, within the `href` attribute.
    d) by a # followed by name, within the `target` attribute.

9) An in-page anchor is dropped with

    a) `<a name='anchor_name'>`.
    b) `<a name='#anchor_name'>`.
    c) `<a name='anchor_name'></a>`.

10) The HTML named character entities can be used for

    a) fractions ¼, ½ and ¾.
    b) fractions of an inch down to 1/16 increments.
    c) fractions in halves, thirds and quarters.

8 Link to the World

Our project goal in this chapter is to get your site linked to the rest of the World-Wide Web, which will not be hard. We also have a lot of other items to cover.

We'll begin with XHTML, which was once the HTML dialect that was going to take over from HTML. (It didn't; it won't.) Then we'll resume coverage of our village of engineers (maybe just you!) that we started in Chapter 7. We'll also cover websites you'll want to know as we transition to HTML 5, and we'll show you some more meta tags that you might want in your head sections. Then we'll cover forms and frames, two topics that don't affect your current project, but will be big in your future if you go deeper into frontend engineering.

So let's get started. Begin by opening to your Companion page.

Online: Knowits > HTML I > Online > 8

History—HTML Was X-Rated

HTML was based on SGML, the Standard Generalized Markup Language, that is an ISO (International Standards Organization) standard for defining markup languages. SGML started the elegantly simple tagging (the `<tag>` opens and `</tag>` closes an element) that made HTML so accessible to so many users.

XML (eXtensible Markup Language) is another markup that has become popular, especially with large businesses sharing data. Near the beginning of this century, an XML-based version of HTML was proposed, standardized and slated to take over from HTML as the official markup language of the World-Wide Web. Unfortunately, XHTML was, in many ways, a silly demotion from much that was good in HTML.

For example, in HTML most tags had corresponding closing tags: `<tag>` was closed by `</tag>`. Some tags, such as `<br>` (for a line break) had no use for a closing tag. In XHTML the closing tag was always required. When it made no sense, it was signaled by a space/slash pair inside the tag's end. `<br>` became `<br />`; an image changed from `<img attrs...>` to `<img attrs... />`.

Probably the height of the foolishness was achieved in attributes such as the "disabled" status of an input:

```
<input . . . disabled> became <input . . .
disabled='disabled'>.
```

The only good news for HTML writers was that the tags and attributes were not documented separately in the XHTML standards (1 and 1.1). Those standards incorporated the HTML 4.01 tags and attributes by reference to the HTML 4.01 Recommendation. A simple translation program can do most of the work of turning valid HTML 4.01 into valid XHTML (and another such program can translate back again).

XHTML did not offer any real advantage that would have made the extra work rewarding. (It still survives today for the environments where web pages are transmitted as files in systems that require XML. It is obsolete, though still possible, where WWW servers serve pages to browsers.)

Your companion page links to deeper discussions of SGML and XHTML.

Websites—Backend

The backend of a website is, to define it loosely, the part that runs on a server if it's job is more complex than the one performed by your hard disk. In a shopping site, for example, the user visits your department store and clicks on Ladies Clothing. The server looks up the topic in the database and prepares pages full of the latest fashions. Later on, the visitor places garments into her shopping cart and then goes to the checkout counter. More data (her purchase details, credit card information and so on) go into the database and physical merchandise gets packaged and put on a truck en route to her home.

The backend engineers use two or more languages. They use a primary language to manipulate data coming from and going to the visitors' browsers. They probably also use SQL (Structured Query Language) to enter and retrieve database data. They will also be pretty good with HTML and CSS, as many of the backend tools require feeding HTML pages to the browsers.

Like HTML, SQL comes in many flavors, one flavor for each database. Unlike frontend engineers, who worry about all the browsers that the visitors might use, the backend engineers have picked a database and only worry about a single SQL dialect.

Languages used on the backend vary widely. Traditional general-purpose languages, such as C++ and Java, are often used. They are good choices for large websites. Google, for instance, uses C++ to receive and respond to your search questions. Java is the primary language for many large enterprises and they are happy to use it to leverage their existing engineering expertise (which is mostly in Java systems). PHP is much simpler if the goal is simply connecting browsers to databases. (Sometimes criticized for its simplicity, PHP was Facebook's primary language for years and still powers giant sites, such as Wikipedia.) Other languages, including Python and Ruby, have enthusiastic adherents on the backend.

If you go beyond informational websites, you will either be working with backend engineers, or you will learn SQL and a backend language to do your own backend engineering.

Tools—caniuse and google

We are now nearing the end of the HTML 4 era and we are someplace in the beginning of the HTML 5 era. You will regularly see HTML 5's latest tags and attributes getting fulsome praise as some author discovers just what great things you can do with the latest.

Often, the praise is excessive and what you "can" do may be really what you "will be able to" do, just as soon as some of the older browsers catch up. One of the best places to ask the question, "can I use..." is at caniuse.com. (There are clickable links on the Companion page).

caniuse

Suppose you think the new progress meters (such as "% completed" bars) are a neat feature and you could use them on your site. Is HTML5 ready? The caniuse.com report (autumn, 2012) is that 40% of today's browsers fully support this feature and just under 12% provide partial support. (That's 52% with no support, if your calculator's not handy. P.S. Near 100%, September, 2013.)

Sadly, you would conclude that this great new feature is not quite ready for prime time. (See also the additional link to our own report on the Companion page. We predict it will be years before you can use this HTML 5 feature.)

google

The verb, "google" now means "conduct a web search" with a search engine. Most people prefer to google with the search engine provided by Google, the company. Other options have their fans, too. We refer to the activity, not a particular company, when we don't capitalize the word.

There are lots of information sources other than caniuse.com and we use many of them constantly. For example, google for HTML 5 information and you will find the HTML5Rocks website. (Yes, a good source for fulsome praise. Don't forget to "caniuse" their recommendations,.)

Head—Meta 2

This is the second of three consecutive chapters, completing the discussion of the head section of the page with meta tags. Chapter 7 showed the vital tags that you probably wanted in your template. You may want to add some of these.

```
<meta name=... content=...>
```

```
<meta name='copyright' content='your
copyright notice'>
```

Add your copyright notice. It may include the named character entity: `&copy;`.

```
<meta name='robots' content='all'>
```

The content may specify `index` or `noindex`. The former directs robots (a search engine crawler) to include the current page in the index. The latter asks that the page not be included. Note that this is a direction to legitimate search engines. Malware will certainly ignore it.

The content may also specify `follow` or `nofollow` (separated by a comma from the `index` or `noindex` specification). This directs the robot to follow, or not, links found in the current page. Again, malware will ignore this direction.

All the search engines have additional, engine-specific tags which you can look up on their owners' sites. Google's crawler is a "googlebot," for example. If you choose, that's `<meta name='googlebot' ...>`.

```
<meta name="zipcode" content="12345,
12346, 12348" >
```

One authoritative site we visit says that this is useless.
Another says we might also try `name=city` and `state` and
`country` tags. Be our guest. We're pretty sure it won't hurt.

```
<meta http-equiv=...
    content=...>
```

Now, here's a small portfolio of `http-equiv` meta tags.

```
<meta http-equiv='content-language'
    content='en-us, fr'>
```

Try the `content-language` tag if your site uses more than
one language.

```
<meta http-equiv="content-script-type"
content="text/JavaScript">
<meta http-equiv="content-style-type"
content="text/CSS">
```

The idea is that with a `content-script-type` you could
just use a `<script>` tag, instead of needing to use
`<script type='text/JavaScript'>`. Of course,
`text/JavaScript` is now the accepted default, so you can
omit it. Of course, the W3C validators (Chapter 7, Tools—
Validators) refuse to accept your markup if you do omit it.
(As noted before, we're not big fans of the W3C validators.)

```
<meta http-equiv='refresh'
content='time; URL'>
```

Two distinct purposes here. First, the page will be refreshed
after `time` seconds. Second, the refresh will load the page
at the specified URL (reload the current page, if no redirect

URL is provided). This can be used to put a "redirecting you to the new address..." page where an old one (possibly embedded in visitors' bookmarks) was located.

Blocks—Forms, Frames

These blocks are of no concern for an information-only website. They are vitally important for websites with backend databases, and for web applications. Adjust your reading speed accordingly.

Forms

You place user input widgets into forms (if you like). Input widgets (next topic) are ones such as `<input type='password' … >`. You can, if you like, place input widgets outside of forms, too, but the form makes collecting information from the widgets and sending it to a backend server much easier. If you use more than one form in your site, you'll want to provide a name for each one. Just enclose your widgets as this shows:

```
<form name='visitor_data'>
… (widgets here)
</form>
```

Frames—`<frameset>` Based Pages

Framesets are very much out of favor. They are a nightmare for non-visual browsers. They are dropped from HTML 5. Don't use them.

Every browser includes a more or less extensive tool set for advanced frontend engineers. Every browser's tool set has been built with frameset technology. Every one. That may tell you something.

Framesets are indispensable for advanced, browser-based applications. We're quite sure that if you make it through Volume V in this series, you will be building frameset-based applications. We'll be building them, too. Do drop us a line with a link to your applications! Thanks.

Frames—Internal (`<iframe>`) Frames

An `iframe` is a window in one page filled with content from a second page. These are prized by malware creators who want, for example, their identity-stealing page to look just like your favorite store's checkout page. Sadly, it's not hard.

Please look up `iframes` when you have a legitimate use for a window within your page into another page. They are well within the capabilities you've already acquired. You might want to use one or two on your project. For instance, you could show a bit of reference information (something beyond lorem ipsum), for example.

Inline—Input Widgets

There are a lot of input widgets to cover. Alternatively, HTML has a pathetically small set of input widgets, that we will cover here. (Widget sets are like that. They are too big until you start using them. Then they never have the widgets you need.) HTML 4, in fact, has a rather small widget set. This is expanding greatly with HTML 5. Use the resources mentioned above to see what you can actually count on having in your visitors' browsers, when you start using input widgets.

There are four separate tags used by HTML 4 widgets: `<button>`, `<input>`, `<select>` and `<textarea>`. The input tag has a `type` attribute that specifies one of ten different (sometimes similar, usually very different) input widgets. You decide how many there are. (Warning, there are several different tags involved in making a `select`— dropdown list—widget.)

`<button>`

A `<button>` is just what you think. It's a thing that you click and it makes something happen.

`<input>`

The most common input widget is a text field. That's where you enter "First Name" and "Last Name," for examples. A `password` widget is a text field that echos asterisks, instead of the characters you type. Other input widgets include radio buttons and checkboxes, file selection widgets, image widgets, and reset and submit buttons. Labels are included too, although they are correctly termed output widgets. (But if you didn't bundle, for example, a "First Name" label with an input text field, your visitor wouldn't know what to do. Often you have to combine widgets to get what you need.)

`<select>`

The `<select>` widget is the common dropdown list box, from which your visitor makes a choice. (Or, it could allow multiple choices.) It is built from `<option>`s. The options may be collected in groups, nicely labeled, for a rather complex, composite widget. Regardless, it's almost always easy to use. (Your UI / UX designer will have an opinion about this! If you are your own UI / UX designer, you should have an opinion about this.)

```
<textarea>
```

A `<textarea>` lets your visitor enter multi-line text. Typical visitor feedback forms provide text areas for comment emails.

Your companion page shows examples:

Online: Knowits > HTML I > Online > 8 "Input Widgets"

Project—Linking Outside

Linking to "foreign" pages (a page is "foreign" if it's not in your website) is very similar to linking to pages in your own site, except that you must provide the "HyperText Transfer Protocol" prefix to the URL:

```
<a href='http://foreign-site.tld'>
```

This is a good time for a more complete description of the URL, the Web's Uniform Resource Locator (aka address).

URL and URI

In the earlier HTML documents you will see the term URI: Uniform Resource Identifier. Formerly, the URL was one type of URI. In later years the URI was no longer distinguished from the URL. Most recently, the URI term is just not used. (Not used except, that is, by geek showoffs with long memories.)

Scheme

In linking to foreign sites, you must provide the "scheme" so the networks will know how to interpret the remainder of the address. The most common scheme on the Web is `HTTP://`. (Or `http://`, if you prefer. The scheme is not case-sensitive.). Another you will see is `https://` (the "secure"—encrypted—version), You may also see `ftp://` (File Transfer Protocol) when you upload files to your ISP. (Many ISPs use just `http://`, even for FTP file transfers.)

Domain

(This is not a full discussion for technical implementers. We are skipping over port numbers and passwords here, for instance.) Next you have a domain, including optional sub-domains, domains and top-level domains. In `mail.google.com`, "mail" is a sub-domain, "google" is a domain and "com" is the top-level domain. Sub-domains are used by large sites that want to break out different messages before they even arrive. Top-level domains (TLDs) used to be just `.com`. `.gov`, `.edu` and, for the military, `.mil`. Today they are commonly used for countries and for domain types, too.

Query String

Do you want to learn more about URLs? Try this one:

```
google.com?q=url
```

That will get you to Google with the topic "url" in the search box. Google returns the SERP (Search Engine Results Page) as if you had navigated to `google.com` and then typed "url" in the search box. If you are wondering, you certainly may put the query string into the `href` of an `<a href=...>` tag.

Fragment Identifier

The "fragment identifier" begins with a # and then continues with the name of an anchor in the page. These are the ones we have been using to navigate to named anchors on our site. Now you know their formal name.

Now that you know all about URLs, go on to the companion page where you will find out how to add an extensive (as extensive as you like) Credits page to your project website.

Online: Knowits > HTML I > Online > 8 "Link to Foreign Sites"

Np++ Secrets—Settings

Click Notepad++. If it has no main menu, press Alt. Now you have a "Settings" menu item. (Alt+S goes to Search. Getting to Settings takes Alt and then a click.) It is, as are many parts of Notepad++, a rich source of choices you can make to get Notepad++ to come out exactly the way you would have made it had you written it yourself.

First, navigate here for the general idea:

Online: Engineers > Frontend Tools >

Notepad++ > More Np++ > Settings

That suggests tools such as Preferences. Try the General tab. Do you want each open file to have a closing "X" on its tab? (We prefer double click to close. Saves tab bar space.) Is the status bar worth a single line of vertical space? Did you know that you could drag tabs off the tab bar and drop them on empty desktop space? (You get another Notepad++ window. You can drag/drop files between Notepad++ windows. You can try other applications, too.)

And that's just one tab of the Preferences dialog. Explore!

On Settings you can click Shortcut Mapper. Start here for a brief discussion:

Online: Engineers > Frontend Tools > Notepad++ > Shortcuts

It seems that we never stop finding new features hiding under Notepad++'s modest exterior. Whenever you need a break, this is a good place to go just to have a look around.

Entities—Dashes

The first, narrowest, dash is technically not even called a dash. It's the hyphen on your keyboard. No character entity required. There are two dashes you will want to make your friends: the en dash and the em dash. The latter is the wide one you see in the heading above.

An em dash is traditionally as wide as the capital "M" letter. The en dash is half the width of the em dash, or the width of the capital "N" letter. Modern type designers do not feel bound by these rules.

If you are a stickler for good grammar, you'll want to follow the links on the Companion page. You wouldn't want to go around using em dashes when you really need en dashes or hyphens, would you? After all, nice people don't do those things!

Quiz

Choose the word or phrase that best completes each sentence.

1) XHTML was based on
   a) SGML.
   b) SGML via HTML.
   c) HTML and XML.
   d) all of the above.

2) In XHTML
   a) tags without closing tags had to close themselves (`<tag />`).
   b) attributes needed values (`<tag disabled='disabled'>`).
   c) attribute values needed to be within quotes (`<tag width='1'>`).
   d) all of the above.

3) Backend engineers are fluent in
   a) PHP.
   b) SQL.
   c) SQL plus at least one other language.

4) HTML 5 is
   a) generally available in modern browsers.
   b) only partially implemented in modern browsers.
   c) the current standard for modern browsers.

5) Framesets are
   a) an impediment to accessibility for the visually impaired.
   b) an organization used by browser vendors.
   c) a viable option for web applications.
   d) all of the above.

6) Meta commands
    a) are not needed when the servers are configured correctly.
    b) are ignored by search engines.
    c) may override server's page headers.
    d) are no longer used.

7) Input widgets
    a) must be used in forms.
    b) may be built from other widgets.
    c) each use a different tag.
    d) require label attributes.

8) URL components include
    a) schemes.
    b) domains.
    c) fragment identifiers.
    d) all of the above.

9) Links to anchors within pages are done with
    a) URL schemes.
    b) top-level domains (TLDs).
    c) URL fragment identifiers.
    d) URL query strings.

10) In HTML you separate values in a range with
    a) a hyphen.
    b) two consecutive hyphens.
    c) an en dash.
    d) an em dash.

9 Finishing Touches

In Chapter 8, XHTML had elbowed its way into the standards process and was about to replace good old HTML. Will HTML be rescued?

In addition, we also get fancy tables (you will need them for a first-rate time line page); we get more meta tags and a number of other topics. To whet your appetite we will list all the wonderful input widgets that HTML 5 promises to bring us.

Begin by turning to your Companion page.

Online: Knowits > HTML I > Online > 9

Next, we resume the history of HTML.

History—HTML Rescued

In 2004 a group of W3C standards participants formed a competing standards efforts. They were not happy with the pace of the HTML 5 standards effort (nothing major had been achieved since 1997's HTML 4). They were also unhappy with the trend toward replacing HTML with XHTML. They forced an acronym on their new group: the Web Hypertext Application Technology Working Group, WHATWG.

The WHATWG membership included all the major browser implementers excepting Microsoft, which was invited but declined to participate. It's first major success was in redefining the public perception that XHTML was the successor to HTML. The opinion of its members, that HTML was not well-served by being forced into an XML mold, has prevailed.

The structure of this group is a bit odd. The editor listens to the discussion and then makes a final determination as to the content of the standard. (The editor serves at the pleasure of the members, who can replace him if they disapprove of his decisions.) This dictatorial approach disqualifies the group's output from consideration as a formal (ISO, for example) standard but it otherwise seems to work well.

WHATWG has abandoned the earlier major revisions scheme, instead calling their document the HTML Living Standard.

Until mid-2012, the WHATWG editor, Ian Hickson, (who kindly agreed to an interview for this knowit) was also the W3C's HTML 5 editor. The tag and attribute specifications in the HTML 5 standard and in the Living Standard were the same. (Not similar: the same. Even the section numbering is identical. In our online tables the "HTML 5" name applies to both.) For the HTML author concerned with writing valid HTML this means that there is just one standard (after HTML 4.01).

`http://wiki.whatwg.org/wiki/FAQ` WHATWG FAQ

Post Script: The W3C has now reformed its HTML5 group, minus editor Hickson and is planning for a 2014 formal adoption of HTML5.

Websites—Frontend

Our first "Frontend Engineers" section, in Chapter 7, covered the designers whose work, at least in theory, precedes the actual coding. This time, we are broadening the definition of "engineer" to include programmers. Unlike the "village" of specialists participating in website design—information architects, UI/UX specialists, designers and SEO experts—we now come to the folks we know best (we are them!), the guys and gals with sleeves rolled up, banging on keyboards to make websites happen.

We all know HTML. We all know how supposedly "standard" HTML looks and acts in different browsers because we all develop with lots of browsers open.

After HTML we know CSS (Volume II, this series). And after that we master the JavaScript language (Volumes III, IV and V).

For those whose brains are large, there are also libraries and frameworks. The jQuery library is very popular (as are its progeny, such as jQuery UI). There is no lack for alternatives, such as Dojo and YUI.

And if that does not cause the grey matter to register a "halt!" then we learn the APIs of the various websites to which ours might link: Facebook, Twitter, Linkedin and so on.

If that's still not enough, we are wrestling with device profusion. Our websites may be viewed on desktop monitors or on laptops, notebooks, tablets (large and small) and smart phones (smaller still). These may have keyboards, mice, screens that you touch and/or GPS inputs. Did we mention inertial inputs (like game controllers you swing to drive a golf ball)?

Well, we'd say more about this but we've got to go on to learn about Scalable Vector Graphics (part of HTML 5) and the 2D canvas element (also part of HTML 5). We don't do much math, so we'll let others figure out Math ML (yet another part of HTML 5) for their equations.

Summary: it's probably easier than ever to build a website for your youth soccer team. That's a good thing. Everyone should be able to create their own online content. But the professional's job is getting larger at an exponential rate. Well, let's be philosophical. That probably means that salaries won't be going down any time soon.

Tools—Screen Capture

So how do you take a nice photo of something on the screen? You use a screen capture utility. It's job is the same as a camera's job, but it works from the opposite side of the screen.

A camera would take a picture of what you see. A screen capture utility makes a copy of the bits inside the computer that become what you see. What's the difference? Quality. A screen capture copies the bits. If you display a screen capture next to the original you won't be able to see the difference. In fact, there won't be any difference. Both will be showing you the exact same bits.

Screen capture utilities are undergoing a transformation. It used to be enough to show a static picture. Well, 2D is giving way to 3D. Today's screen capture utilities vie with each other to create the best full-motion pictures of whatever happens on your screen.

We use an old utility, very good at 2D but barely able to do 3D. We wouldn't pick it again. Soon we'll google for more recent alternatives and then we'll put a recommendation on the Companion page. For now, you, too, have to google for screen capture.

Head—Meta 3

Here we go again! This is your third, and final, installment of meta tags for your head section. Again, you might find one or two of these that you will add to your template so they always come along (even when you have a very bad day).

name

```
<meta name="revised" content="31
December, 2012">
```

How do you tell a visiting search engine whether it has indexed the latest version of your page? This is the one.

```
< meta name="revisit-after" content="30
days">
```

How do you invite a search engine to come back for another visit? This is the one.

```
<meta name="reply-to" content="email
address">
```

How do you tell a reader savvy enough to View Source how to get in touch? (And how do you tell spammers where to find you?) This is the one.

http-equiv

```
<meta http-equiv='cache-control'
content='no-cache'>
```

Some search engines will keep copies of your pages in cache. This is generally their issue, not yours. If, however, your page is updated hourly (or by the minute) you can try this one to stay out of cache.

```
<meta http-equiv='pragma' content='no-
cache'>
```

If you see this one, it is just an earlier (and less-readable) form of the one above.

```
<meta http-equiv='expires' content='GMT
time string'>
```

How do you tell a search engine not to show your page forever? This is the one. You will have to look up the GMT time string format. It must be followed exactly. Search engine crawlers are not very imaginative.

Blocks—Fancy Tables

Ready to get fancy with that time line? These are your tools.

Row and Column Spans

You have a table of historical figures. You might organize it this way:

Person 1	Date born	Place born
	Date of death	Place of death
Person 2	Date born	Place born
	Date of death	Place of death

Or you might organize the table this way:

	Birth		Death	
	Date	Place	Date	Place
Person 1				
Person 2				

In the first example, your person names span two rows. In the second, the column heads "Birth" and "Death" both span two columns. Your Companion page will show you how to do this in HTML.

Columns

HTML has tables divided into rows that are divided into cells. Columns? Well, you had to do it one way or the other. If you really want to introduce actual columns (not just cells that happen to align vertically), you can.

Column Groups

And once you start working with columns, you will want to group them. (See the example table with the two-column headings.) HTML can do this, too.

Turn to your Companion page for explanations, examples and exercises.

Online: Knowits > HTML I > Online > 9

Inline—HTML 5 Widgets

Don't we want all these widgets! Some we could use right now and others we're pretty sure will come in handy soon enough. Too bad that tools like "caniuse" are such pessimists!

Color

A good color chooser takes days to write. (Picture one with three sliders, for red, green and blue, zero through 255 and a big sample area that changes colors as you slide them.) This would be great.

Date, datetime, datetime-local

What day would your visitor like that appointment? What time? Is that local time or GMT?

Email

One of the toughest jobs in JavaScript is to validate an email address. Being able to drop in an HTML email input widget would save days.

Keygen

For the secure application, this one automates key generation for public/private key security applications.

Month

What month would you like that appointment for your checkup?

Number

Today, you use a text field. Then you write some JavaScript to at least ensure that the field contains all digits.

Output

An output field in the shopping application could contain an order total. JavaScript could compute it from the order details. This one will simplify the programming.

Range

You've asked for a number from 1 through 10. Think about the logic involved in validating input from text fields for ten. Is the input one or two characters long? If it's two long, is it "10"? If it's one long, is a digit from "1" through "9"? It's not rocket science, but it's certainly tedious.

Search

Did you want to prepare for a google? This is your widget.

Tel

Yes, that's the telephone number, another item that we get in text fields today. Wouldn't it be great to have a widget that ensured a correctly formatted phone number? (Think about the issues if your visitors might not be located in your native country. Do you know the format of a phone number in Bulgaria? In Burkina Faso? Burma? Burundi? And those are just the "Bu" countries.)

Time

Your application how has a visitor who wants an appointment next Tuesday. Great. What time on Tuesday?

URL

Last chapter we explained the format of a URL, leaving out lots of details. You may remember that it's an optional scheme, followed by optional sub-domains, a domain name, a top-level domain, an optional query and an optional fragment identifier. A widget that could validate web addresses would save hours and hours of programming.

Week

Of course we'll be happy to give you an appointment. What week would be convenient?

Yes, we really think every one of these input widgets will find a place in our tool kits. Now, if only the browser folks would hurry up and get them implemented!

Project—Title and Time Line

Well, so much for looking forward to what we'll have tomorrow. Time to work with what we have today. Before we send you off to the Companion page, let's give a moment's thought to your home page. To a web marketer this is a "landing page" which must compel your visitor to dig deeper.

If you were writing a book, this would be your cover. Think about book covers. Your potential reader might have researched your topic on the Web, might have gone to Amazon and read the reader reviews, might have decided to buy your book. That's great! The cover only needs to have the title and your name, to reassure the reader that this is, in fact, the right book.

But what about the browser in the bookstore? He or she is attracted by your cover's color and graphics. The front cover is the landing page. You want your browser (the human, not the software) to turn the book over and read the back cover, where you make a pitch. The back cover pitch must be so compelling that your browser looks inside your book, or marches straight to the counter to buy it. That is the way you want to be thinking about your home page.

Your time line is an information page. You want it to convey a clear picture. (In our sample, we want you to see that Galileo came early in the century, Newton came late.) And if you can make the time line good looking, you'll have a screen shot that will make good cover art.

Ready? The Companion page will tell you all you need to know to make the sort of fancy tables that will tell your story, and help make a compelling cover:

Online: Knowits > HTML I > Online > 9 "Time Lines"

Motto for website builders: "They're all landing pages."

Np++ Secrets—Blocks

Sometimes you'll want to work with blocks (2D rectangles) of text. Notepad++ makes the most common tasks, indenting and outdenting lines, part of its bread and butter. (Highlight the lines, then press Tab or Shift+Tab). But what if you don't want to move whole lines?

Well, you can move any block around the screen. Here's how:

> Online: Engineers > Frontend Tools >
>
> Notepad++ > More Np++ > BlockMode

Entities—HTML

If you prepare web pages about the preparation of web pages, you have to be able to show an HTML tag: `<tag>`. But your browser, if you feed it `<tag>` will think that you have an HTML tag and will try to use it as one. How do you trick it into showing a tag?

You replace the opening < with the character entity for the "less than" sign: `&lt;`. Then you show a tag as: `&lt;tag>`.

How do you show how to write a character entity? `&yen;` will show a yen sign. To show the characters you type to get a yen sign, you substitute the character entity for the ampersand: `&amp;yen;`. Now your browser substitutes the ampersand for the `&amp;` and it shows "¥" on the screen.

Perhaps you'll never have occasion to use these. We'll not mention them on the quiz.

Online: Knowits > HTML I > Online > 9 "Character Entities"

Quiz

Choose the word or phrase that best completes each sentence.

1) The Web Hypertext Application Technology Working Group
    a) saved HTML from becoming XHTML.
    b) wrote the HTML 5 specification.
    c) included all the major browser vendors.
    d) created a competing set of HTML tags and attributes.

2) Frontend programmers know
    a) HTML.
    b) how different browsers render HTML.
    c) HTML, CSS and JavaScript.
    d) all of the above.

3) Frontend programmers may also know
    a) libraries, such as jQuery.
    b) APIs to work with sites like Facebook and Twitter.
    c) different device inputs, such as mice and touch.
    d) all of the above, and lots more, too!

4) Using a screen capture utility is
    a) as good as using an inexpensive digital camera.
    b) as good as using a professional digital camera.
    c) better than either of the above.

5) Meta tags let HTML
    a) control search engine crawlers.
    b) provide information for search engine crawlers.
    c) tell servers how to form HTML page headers.

6) Table cells
    a) are defined with `<tc>` tags.
    b) provide content for the intersection of a single row and column.
    c) may span multiple rows with a `<rowspan>` tag.
    d) may span multiple rows with a `rowspan` attribute.

7) HTML lets you define column groups with
    a) a `<colspan>` tag.
    b) `<column>` tags.
    c) `<colgroup>` tags.
    d) `<td>` attributes.

8) Your website home page is a type of
    a) landing page.
    b) book front cover.
    c) book front and back cover.
    d) all of the above.

9) HTML 5 input widgets include:
    a) week, color and telephone numbers.
    b) date, GMT datetime and local datetime.
    c) email addresses and website URLs.
    d) all of the above.

10) (Research project) Tables can be nested within `<td>` tags
    a) in specialized browsers.
    b) in some major browsers.
    c) in Chrome, Firefox, MSIE and Opera

10 Go Live!

Welcome to the tenth and final chapter. By now you know a thing or two about HTML, right? It's probably easier than you guessed. Here we are mostly finishing up. We'll bring our history up to the minute, have a final word on SEO and give you a run down on what great new blocks you'll get as soon as HTML 5 is ready for prime time. We'll also tidy up some loose ends, making sure we send you off into the brave world with every tag you can use today and tomorrow. Last, and by no means least, we'll share some ideas about launching your site.

Turn to the Companion page, and let's get started.

History—HTML 5

Today we live caught in time between HTML 4.01 and HTML 5. To be more exact, we are caught between the tags and attributes of HTML 4.01 and the tags and attributes of HTML 5, which are also the tags and attributes of the HTML Living Standard. This should not be a problem, but it is.

In desktop browsers, there is substantial HTML 4 compatibility between the standards-based group: Chrome, Firefox, Opera and Safari, and the Microsoft browsers, MSIE 8 and later.

Most browsers have automatic update programs. Chrome has been the most aggressive (and most successful). If you had installed an early test version (Chrome 0.6, for example) you would today have the latest production Chrome (version 23, as of late 2012—version 29, September, 2013) and you would never have seen a "Do you want to upgrade?" message. The rest of the non-MSIE browsers are now similarly updated quietly.

Not so with the Microsoft browsers. MSIE 9, for example, has been programmed not to run on the still-popular Windows XP operating system, so there is a definite break between the partly-HTML 5 MSIE 9 and the entirely-HTML 4.01 MSIE 8.

Bottom line: you can use HTML 4.01 tags and attributes and not worry. Alternatively, you can use HTML 5 and not support some MSIE browsers. So you will know which, our knowit-specific supplemental tables are here:

Online: Knowits > HTML I > Tables

The "Tags/Attrs" table lists the HTML tags that are part of both the HTML 4.01 and the HTML 5 standards, and the attributes of those tags that are also part of both standards. These enjoy almost complete support in today's browsers.

15,000 megayears ago the universe was born. 15,000 grandpayears ago, *homo sapiens* hunted and gathered. 15,000 days ago, the Internet was born. 15,000 hours ago, Facebook was a small, private company. We predict that HTML will be more dominant in the next decade than it was in the last. And we fearlessly predict that people will commonly use it for activities not yet invented.

`http://www.w3counter.com/trends` Ongoing browser wars.

`http://www.martinrinehart.com/pages/genealogy-programming-languages.html` Languages are long-lived.

Websites—Credits

We began our discussions of "Websites" with an introduction to SEO. Here, we'll finish with another discussion of SEO. This time, we'll talk about links. Let's back up to the late 1990s. Two Stanford students, Sergey Brin and Larry Page, noticed that outbound links (the ones in href attributes in the HTML) were easy to follow but inbound links (the ones in href attributes on other sites' HTML) were invisible. "What could we learn," they asked themselves, "if we knew about the inbound links?"

They thought they might learn just how important a site was by studying its inbound links. So they set a Stanford server to work crawling the web, logging links. Eventually, they had every server Stanford could spare (and, some said, servers that Stanford couldn't spare) crawling the web, logging links.

This project started turning out search rankings that were a lot better than the best then available. It turned into a company called Google and its founders amassed fortunes that are huge, even by the standards of Silicon Valley success stories.

Today, if you want a top Google ranking, the inbound links to your site are gold. To get inbound links, the sure strategy is to be the best site on the web in whatever your specialty. You can nudge your visibility along with your outbound links.

So never pass up the opportunity to link to another site. Follow up every outbound link with a "Thank You" email. If the outbound link is to a site relevant to yours, your site should be relevant to theirs. And if your site is, in fact, the best site in your field, the inbound links will follow. Google's web crawlers will find your site and recognize it as the very first they should list for searchers inquiring about your specialty.

One other thing: this strategy requires patience. While you are waiting, keep working on your site. Be the best.

Yet another thing: there are "link farms" which will, for a price, link to your site, regardless of content. These can give you a dramatic, instant success story. Google warns against using them, however. When Google's crawlers discover that all your inbound links are from link farms they blackball your site and it will be years before you will be listed on even the very last page of search results.

Give credits and link to the other good sites in your field.

Tools—Minifier and FTP

Minifier

Many people run their sites through a program called a "minfier" that compresses pages without losing any content. The best results are obtained from minifying JavaScript. HTML is not so squishy. You may want to minify your site before you upload it to your Internet Service Provider (ISP). Your ISP may minify your pages before it serves them, so you don't need to do this yourself. Ask your ISP.

FTP Utility

How do you send a file to your ISP? Most ISPs have a web app that you run. It will have an `<input type='file'...>` tag. You browse for your file on your disk and a click or three later, your file is on its way to your ISP. (Backend programming courtesy of the ISP, and we love them for it!)

If you are going to send more than a few files you will want to have an FTP utility. This stands for the pre-WWW File Transfer Protocol that was used for sending a file from one computer to another (mainframes back then). A command-line utility let you enter the commands that initiated the transfer process.

This old technology stills exists and is still used. The number of people who know the commands for raw FTP transfers is dwindling. The rest of us use an FTP program. This is like two Windows Explorer programs that run side by side. In one you see files on your system. The other shows the files on the remote system. You highlight a file or folder on your local system, another on the remote system and click! The file is transferred. (Many also work by drag and drop.)

We don't suggest you rush to acquire a good FTP utility. We do suggest that you remember this is an option. When clicking on your ISP's file app becomes tedious, then you have reached the point where you will want to get an FTP utility.

Head—Your Favicon

A favicon is that little square, 16 by 16 pixels, that you see next to a site name in a tab in your browsers. If the favicon is a good one, it will remind you of its site, even when you are actually viewing a site three browser tabs removed. Your browsers may also include the favicons in your bookmarks (hence the name: FAVorites ICON).

There are two steps required to have a favicon for your own site:

1. Create a 16 by 16 pixel graphic.

2. Link it to your pages.

The first step is very difficult. We suggest you enlist the aid of all your friends and relations. Any good idea may be the one that solves the puzzle. It is hard to capture a site's essence in 16 by 16 pixels. Once you have a design in mind, any good art program will do the job. Even a lame one like MS Paint. The Companion page links to online favicon services that have editors that will eliminate the need for another art program.

Just don't be surprised, however, when you find that your brilliant idea doesn't really work at 16 by 16. It would be much more surprising if it DID work. If there is a secret to having a good favicon, it's this: be a ruthless critic, recklessly unafraid to throw out failed attempts. If you're not mad at yourself before you get a good favicon, you're being too timid.

With your graphic ready, linking it to your pages is simple. The Companion page explains how:

Online: Knowits > HTML I > Online > 10 "Favicon"

Blocks—HTML 5

HTML 5 adds, or will add, lots of new blocks to your tool kit. Be sure you stop by a site like caniuse.com before you add any of these today, however.

Structure

Least glamorous of the new capabilities, HTML 5 adds a huge increment to your ability to structure your pages for the precise needs of your content.

<article>

You will be able to create pages that contain multiple articles, wrapping each article in <article> and </article> tags.

<aside>

The "aside" lets you digress a bit. With CSS you can style an aside as a sidebar, adding a bit of colorful commentary without interrupting the main flow,

<details>

For those with an insatiable appetite for more knowledge (our kind of people!) you can provide additional details. CSS will let you provide a separate style.

`<figcaption>`

Figures should have captions. At a minimum they should have a number that lets your text have an in-text reference, such as "As Figure 3.2 shows...".

`<figure>`

Of course, figure captions without figures don't make very much sense, do they?

`<footer>`

You may have have a page footer, or you may have a footer for each article, if your page is divided into multiple articles.

`<header>`

And if you have footers, you will also want headers, of course.

`<hgroup>`

There are times when you want to follow an `<h2>` heading immediately with an `<h3>`. This is not a happy combination if the pagination splits the two. An `<hgroup>` will let you keep these together.

`<section>`

If you can have multiple articles, you may also want to divide long ones into multiple sections. HTML 5 gives you tremendous flexibility in organizing your pages.

`<summary>`

By coincidence, the `<summary>` comes last in this alphabetical grouping of structuring blocks. As with headers and footers, you can apply summaries to articles, sections or whatever your content requires.

Drawing

Canvas

First introduced by Apple, the canvas lets you paint within your HTML page. You can do amazing, never-before-seen work on the canvas. This tag will be a good topic for an entire book.

SVG

Scalable Vector Graphics are another alternative for painting directly within your HTML page. "Graphics" means things you draw (lines, circles, stars, whatever you can dream). "Vector" means that your drawing is done with lines: draw from bottom-left up to right-center... The advantage of vectors is that they will render correctly on your phone and on the stadium's megatron. "Scalable" refers to this size flexibility. This tag is another good topic for an entire book.

Media

Probably the most dramatic of the new HTML 5 capabilities are the different "block" tags that really go beyond visual media.

<audio>

Just what it says, here we add sound. Would you like a sound clip when the page loads? Perhaps your visitor wants to listen to Beethoven's 5th Symphony? (Check carefully that the browsers you want to support are compatible with your audio file types.)

<progress>

A progress meter is a good idea to show your visitor where you are in the audio or video (or prosaic things, like download progress). We have some negative thoughts, however, on today's progress widgets. (See the Companion page.)

`<source>`

You do want to be able to play your own music tracks behind another video track, don't you? With `<source>` you will be able to specify as many sources as you need.

`<track>`

The concept of tracks is well supported with audio CDs. You want to bring user control over the tracks forward to controls your visitor can manipulate. This would be nice for video, too.

`<video>`

Yes, the world is going video. The WWW is going video, too. We expect we'll be using lots of `<video>` as soon as its support grows a bit. We expect that you will, too.

Multilingual

Probably less fun than any of the other areas, the support for more languages is critically important to those who use the languages affected.

`<bdi>`

Bidirectional text does not impact western languages. But what if you were writing Arabic, or Hebrew, for examples, and wanted to include an English word? The convention is to include the foreign word, written in its left-to-right direction, within your right-to-left text.

`<rp>`, `<rt>`, `<ruby>`

With due apologies to those who use East Asian languages, we confess to not understanding these three. Those who know tell us that they correct some serious deficiencies in

HTML's ability to render languages such as Chinese, Japanese and Korean.

Other

<command>

A concept from Java that may become a vital part of all menu choices, it will not, however, worry the non-JavaScripters.

<embed>

There is no possibility that any standard could encompass all the different things that you might want on the web. The <embed> command, being renewed in HTML 5, has appeared in earlier HTML versions as a means of including yet-to-be-invented content. (It has never been more than—ahem, we'll be kind—modestly successful. Will this be different?)

<mark>

This tag lets you mark a section of a quote for reference in your text.

<menu>

Now the province of JavaScript (and, to a lesser extent, of fancy CSS tricks) menus will have direct support at some future point.

<meter>

Like the <progress> tag, the meter lets you display numeric values graphically. (As with <progress> we have some negative thoughts, pointed out on the Companion page.)

`<nav>`

Most pages have a navigation area; some have more than one. You will be able to mark your navigation areas appropriately with this tag.

`<time>`

This proposed tag lets you provide a machine-readable time stamp, separate from the time you show to your visitors, which could be, for example, a clock on the wall. Using a correct `<time>` will let web crawlers and non-visual browsers read the time.

`<wbr>`

The opposite of the non-breaking space, the `<wbr>` (Word BReak) is inserted into long "words" where, you tell the browser, the "word" might be broken to wrap lines intelligently. This might be used at strategic locations in a URL, for example.

Potpourri

Keen-eyed readers will immediately see that this section is located where the "Inline" section lives in the other chapters. We have a handful of both block and inline elements that didn't fit in any of the earlier chapters, which we mention here before we come to the end of this knowit.

Block

The `<object>` and its companion `<param>` allow the inventors of new types of content to have a formal place to put them. In older days, these tags contained Java applets. Tomorrow's objects might have more staying power.

Inline

The `<bdo>` tag (Bi-Directional Override) is for those who use left-to-right reading words in right-to-left reading text.

The `<cite>` tag allows you to insert citations to sources (such as for quotations) in your text. (Correct formatting is up to you.)

The `<dfn>` tag (definition) can surround definitions of terms if you will be defining new terms. Again, correct formatting is up to you.

The `<q>` tag can be used in place of the typewritten pseudo quote marks. The typewriter's single quote is really an apostrophe, (such as the possessive in the word "typewriter's" here). Notice that it would be a bad mark for starting a quote. The typewritten "double quote" is really an inch mark. (See the marks around "double quote" for examples of true quotes that our word processor uses to replace the inch marks we type.) Using the `<q>` tag (no closing tag) in place of the typewritten marks lets your browsers handle this bit of grammar as best they know how.

Warning: Some browsers are smart enough to wrap double quotes around a quotation, and wrap single quotes around a word or phrase within the quotation. Some are not. Test and decide which you prefer. Your choices are correct quotes, but only in smart browsers, or typewriter quotes, never really correct but never badly wrong. There will be no question on this in the quiz, as there is no right answer.

Project—Test, Retest

Ready to upload your project to your ISP? (Or to the website your instructors have been good enough to find at your school?) Give it a final careful check and be sure you click every link on every page. Now upload!

You should be delighted to see your own work coming at you from somewhere in cyberspace. Feels great, doesn't it?

Now the bad news. Give your uploaded site another careful check, And be double sure that you click every link on every page. Links have a funny way of going bad as they travel from your disk to your ISP. No, it's not because the links are getting scrambled. It's because the site builder (that would be you) forgot something.

You did use nothing but lowercase folder and file names, didn't you? You did use full, absolute addressing for foreign sites, didn't you?

Fix the problems. No celebrating yet. Test all the links again. Any problems? Go back to the beginning of this paragraph and keep at it. Five or ten passes would be normal.

Got here? It's perfect! Champagne time! Your site is up-to-the-minute. It's a work of art, by you. Congratulations. It won't need any more work for a while. (Probably not until you drag your groggy self out of bed in the morning, take another look and see that "How could I have missed it?" mistake.) We've been there. Welcome to the World-Wide Web. (No cursing at Sir Tim. It's not his fault.)

Np++ Secrets—Source Viewer

Man is a tool-making animal. In the dim past, some unsung genius discovered that taking a stick with you when you went hunting was a Good Thing. It wasn't long before someone discovered the right kind of stone for making a simple spear head that could be tied onto a stick with strips of animal hide.

Programmers show this heritage. Since the dawn of programming languages (the 1950s) programmers have created tools for themselves. The king of programming tools is called the Integrated Development Environment (IDE). An IDE combines a good programming editor with other tools such as a form painter and a navigable dictionary of all the parts of the program. (A large program is like a large website: it uses many different files.)

And as quickly as we developed IDEs for programming in a language like Java, we also developed multi-lingual programming needs, such as programming the website frontend with HTML, CSS and JavaScript. These are beyond the skill of single-language IDEs. While we wait for the IDEs to catch up we can integrate our editor with our browsers and get quite close to the ease of use of a good IDE. If this volume has gotten you started on frontend programming, either as a vocation or an avocation, integrate your editor with your browsers for a more seamless workflow. You'll be delighted with the result:

Online: Engineers > Frontend Tools > Notepad++ > Source

One sad note: Google Chrome does not, as yet, allow this wonderful integration. Enjoy it in Firefox, MSIE and Opera.

Entities—nbsp, iquest

Moving on, there are western languages in which, for those of us who grew up with English, the question mark is used upside down. If you are one of those who grew up thinking that there were two correct ways to write a question mark, HTML gives you the `&iquest;` (inverted question mark) named character entity.

Our last named character entity is . It stands for Non-Breaking SPace. It's original use was as a space between words that you did not want separated at a line end. Assume that you were abbreviating the United States as the "U. S." but did not want a line break to fall between the "U." and "S.". In HTML that would be U. S..

HTML 5 gives us the <wbr> tag for the opposite use. That's a Word BReak and it is used in long "words" that may need to be broken, but don't have spaces on which to break. (Prime target: URLs.)

> Online: Knowits > HTML I > Online > 10 "Character Entities"

The   is often used by those who don't know CSS to introduce some space to the left of something that they want to indent. In CSS you could just specify the padding you want on the left, and you could specify the exact number of pixels you had in mind, too. Your indenting would be identical, in all browsers. (In case you were wondering if you really wanted to go on to CSS, we thought you'd like to know.)

And congratulations on completing this knowit! See you in Volume II.

 (CSS is only half the size of HTML, and Volume II is only half the size of this Volume. Better, almost half of CSS is right there in the first chapter. You'll find out how to indent, professionally, before you get to Chapter 2.)

Quiz

Choose the word or phrase that best completes each sentence.

1) The coming HTML standard(s) is (are)
   a) the WHATWG Living HTML.
   b) the W3C HTML 5 Recommendation,
   c) Living HTML and HTML 5.
   d) none of the above.

2) The next W3C HTML standard will be
   a) HTML 5, due in 2013.
   b) HTML 5, due in 2013 to replace XHTML.
   c) HTML 5, due in 2013 to replace HTML 4.01 from 1999.
   d) HTML 5, due in 2014 to replace HTML 4.01 from 1999.

3) Buying inbound links from a link farm
   a) may increase your Google rank immediately.
   b) may get your site removed from search results by Google.
   c) both of the above.

4) An FTP program
   a) is necessary to upload your files to your ISP.
   b) is necessary to use FTP commands.
   c) replaces FTP commands.

5) Your site's favicon
   a) is needed to include your site in a "favorites" list.
   b) is a 32 x 32 pixel graphic.
   c) is a 16 x 16 pixel graphic.
   d) is attached to your site, not to specific pages.

6) You should play audio clips via HTML 5 when
    a) your browser successfully plays the audio file.
    b) the browsers you want to support all play the audio file.
    c) you can convert the audio file to a type accepted by the browsers you want to support.

7) You can use HTML 5 headers and footers with
    a) your web pages.
    b) articles within your pages.
    c) sections within your pages and articles.
    d) all of the above.

8) The <bdo> tag is important if
    a) you need to populate Body of Document sections.
    b) you need to write Chinese, bottom-to-top.
    c) you need to mix Aramaic and Arabic languages.
    d) you need to use French words in a Hebrew document.

9) The <cite> and </cite> pair would surround
    a) references to traffic tickets.
    b) new species viewed by bird watchers.
    c) references to source documents for quotations.

10) The   named character entity is a
    a) non-bidirectional spelling.
    b) non-breaking space.
    c) normally bilateral search parameter.

A   Interview, Ian Hickson

Ian Hickson is the author of the WHATWG's Living HTML standard and the author of most of the W3C's HTML5 specification. He is also the author of the widely used Acid test suites (tests that measure how well a browser conforms to the standards).

As an employee of Opera, Hickson was the Editor of the W3C's HTML5 specification. In 2004, when the WHATWG group was formed, Hickson became the Editor of that groups Living HTML standard. He served as editor for both organizations until 2012.

Fortunately, for those of us who write HTML, Hickson was able to keep the specifications identical in the key sections specifying tags and tag attributes. This meant that, as authors, there was only a single standard. This is still substantially true as the W3C incorporates much of the Living HTML standard by license from WHATWG.

Unfortunately, for those of us who write HTML, the W3C decided to complete work on its HTML5 standard using different editors, a decision that was not explained. WHATWG is supported by Apple (Safari), Google (Chrome), Mozilla (Firefox) and Opera. Microsoft was invited to join, but declined. See Appendix B for a list of the W3C's HTML5 editors.

This interview was conducted prior to the WHATWG / W3C split. Hickson's responses are shaded.

How much of the actual writing does the "editor" do?

> More or less all of it.

The WHATWG started in 2004 (five years after HTML 4.01 became a W3C Recommendation and seven years after HTML 4). What was your part in it, back then? Was this before you left Opera?

> Same part as now! This was indeed before I left Opera.

Any frontend engineer has a bellyful of browser incompatibility stories, so we all applaud the standards effort. What got you interested in it?

> I started working on standards back in the late 90s when I tried to make my home page and found none of the browsers followed the specs.

It looks to us like the years tossed around (2022, for one) are far too pessimistic. How long before the W3C HTML5 Editor's Draft becomes a Recommendation?

> You'll have to ask the W3C. In 2007 they said 2010, and in 2011 they said 2014. Personally, I think it's silly to worry about Recommendations – the HTML standard has been doing fine for years without being "finished", so it's time to give up on version numbers and embrace the Web way of continual improvement. That's why on the WHATWG HTML spec we've long stopped referring to it as HTML5; it's now just the HTML living standard.
> http://whatwg.org/html

What do you see as the time frame for `<canvas>`? And SVG?

> Not sure what you mean.

Tell us about the way Microdata and RDF work together (or how we can choose the right one).

> RDF and microdata have little to do with each other. RDF is a data model, a way of storing data.

As such it solves a pretty uninteresting problem.
There are lots of data models, e.g. lists, name-value
pairs, trees... Data models are IMHO just an
implementation detail. There's no need to
standardize them.

Microdata is just a way of annotating HTML to
enable users to publish their structured data as
HTML while keeping it somewhat machine-
readable. (The data model that microdata models is
nested name-value pairs, but that's a minor detail.)

The scripting interface is a major part of the HTML
5 draft standards. Are you working closely with
ECMA TC 39?

Sure. Despite the Web specs being developed using
remarkably open mechanisms—anyone can join in,
propose things, etc—there's really only a small
number of people who really do all the work on all
the various Web standards. This means that there's
almost always people who are on multiple groups
at once, and so it is with the JavaScript and HTML
work. This helps us make sure we all keep going in
roughly the same direction over all.

What are some of the differences between the
WHATWG and the W3C HTML 5 standards?

There aren't any differences worth talking about.
There's some minor editorial things, they're listed
in the WHATWG spec's front matter if you are
curious.
http://www.whatwg.org/specs/web-apps/current-

> work/multipage/introduction.html#how-do-the-whatwg-and-w3c-specifications-differ?

(P. S. The W3C's target, as of late 2012, is 2014.)

The WHATWG and the W3C "standards" do not have ANSI or ISO blessings yet, do they? Does this matter?

> What matters is what gets implemented.

Neither HTML5 standard has a machine-readable meta language spec (for those of us who hack up personal tools). Anything planned?

> Can you elaborate? What do you have in mind?

Microsoft claims to have gotten the standards-based religion but it seems happy to leave pre-standards browser versions at large (especially for Windows XP users). Any insight on how long we'll still have IE 8 and earlier as an anchor?

> You'd have to ask Microsoft.

A while back we downloaded Google Chrome, version 0.6. Now we're up to version 15.x with no updates on our part. Have major version numbers become meaningless?

> Yes.

(P. S. As of November, 2012, Chrome is at version 23.x.)

Are the days of `<noscript>` behind us?

> I sure hope so.

Is Google going to give us SketchUp in the browser?

> For Google-specific questions please contact `press@google.com`.

(P. S. Google's plans for SketchUp, a 3D modeling program, became clear earlier this year. It sold the product to Trimble, a separate company.)

We want touch events! When will they be widespread?

> For DOM Events questions I recommend approaching the editors of the DOM Events specs. I'm not closely involved in the DOM Events work.

And will we ever see them on our desktop monitors?

> I hope not, touching desktop monitors is ergonomically horrible! :-)

For the engineer who hasn't got a month free to read the standards forward (never mind backward) what is the best way to take advantage of these great resources?

> If by "these great resources" you mean the specs, then if you don't have time to read the specs I'm not sure they'll be of much use to you directly. :-)

(P. S. The WHATWG Living HTML specification if printed as a trade paperback, such as this one, would be about 7 inches—18 cm—thick.)

B HTML5 Editors

WHATWG: Ian Hickson

W3C:
> Robin Berjon, W3C
> Travis Leithead, Microsoft
> Erika Doyle Navara, Microsoft
> Edward O'Connor, Apple
> Silvia Pfeiffer

Dr. Pfeiffer heads her own consultancy specializing in Web video.

W3C credits Ian Hickson as "Previous Editor."

C   Answers to Quiz Questions

I	1c, 2d, 3a, 4c, 5b, 6c, 7b, 8b, 9a, 10d
II	1c, 2c, 3c, 4c, 5c, 6c, 7d, 8c, 9d, 10d
III	1c, 2d, 3c, 4d, 5d, 6c, 7c, 8d, 9d, 10d
IV	1c, 2c, 3b, 4d, 5a, 6c, 7d, 8b, 9c, 10c
V	1c, 2a, 3d, 4b, 5d, 6d, 7c, 8d, 9c, 10c
VI	1d, 2a, 3c, 4b, 5d, 6d, 7d, 8b, 9d, 10c
VII	1b, 2c, 3b, 4a, 5c, 6d, 7c, 8c, 9c, 10a
VIII	1d, 2d, 3c, 4b, 5d, 6c, 7b, 8d, 9c, 10c
IX	1a, 2d, 3d, 4c, 5b, 6d, 7c, 8d, 9d, 10c
X	1b, 2d, 3c, 4c, 5c, 6c, 7d, 8d, 9c, 10b

Reference

This knowit print portion is not a reference tool. (Printed matter is not clickable.)

For a quick reference to HTML tags:

> google "html tag reference."

We regularly check our tables against those at W3Schools (and report errors, when we find them). Their default tag index includes HTML5 and deprecated/obsolete earlier tags.

Quackit.com defaults to HTML 4.01. It takes one more click to get their HTML 5 list.

HTMLdog gives you "the latest version of strict XHTML" (which is HTML 4.01, of course).

We recommend bookmarking those you find most helpful. After Chapter 8, you'll be able to build your own HTML reference links page. We use ours constantly (though most of it goes into more advanced topics). One you build for yourself will be the one you really like.

www.ingramcontent.com/pod-product-compliance
Lightning Source LLC
Chambersburg PA
CBHW052145070326
40689CB00050B/2076